How to Understand and Overcome Depression

Earnest Larsen

LIGUORI
PUBLICATIONS

One Liguori Drive
Liguori, Mo. 63057
(314) 464-2500

Imprimi Potest:
Edmund T. Langton, C.SS.R.
Provincial, St. Louis Province
Redemptorist Fathers

Imprimatur:
+John N. Wurm, S.T.D., Ph.D.
Vicar General, Archdiocese of St. Louis

IBSN 0-89243-071-0
Library of Congress Catalog Card Number: 77-90523

Table of Contents

Introduction

Depression and happiness cannot coexist. Anyone who has had even the slightest contact with depression would agree with that statement. Some would make it even stronger: "Right, depression is a blight. I hate it. It ruins everything. But what can be done about it? How can a person avoid depression?"

The problem is that it is so nebulous and vague. "If only it were a wound or a bruise or a broken bone, then I would know what it is. I could look at it, treat it, and be done with the whole thing."

Depression is none of those things, but it is just as real. Some people liken depression to a heaviness of heart. I have heard it described as an ugly mist arising like fog out of a swamp spoiling a sunshiny day. The day might start bright enough, but then something happens. A dark cloud moves in front of the sun. It grows like a thunderhead. The whole sky darkens. And the more worry, the worse it gets.

For some people it is a night fear. The day is finally put to rest, but what of tomorrow? Will it be tinged with sadness, with this heaviness? Will tomorrow be lived in a consuming sense of "gray"? Not really miserable perhaps, but with a nagging sense that all is not right. Will tomorrow be nothing but apprehension and lack of enthusiasm and joy?

There are many ways of speaking of depression. Dr. Leonard Cammer in his book *Up From Depression* begins his foreword with this sentence, "Every one of us is depressed at times and that is perfectly normal."

What Dr. Cammer means is that we have all felt blue or down at times. Probably for most people the feeling passed and they rebounded to a more normal pattern of living.

But there is another type of depression. This is a true disease. It is when there is no rebound, when the melancholia interferes with our ordinary daily tasks. It can so interfere that we become actually paralyzed.

Dr. Cammer states that he finds it useful to classify depression as (1) *endogenous* (a word which literally means internally generated), (2) *reactive* (so named because it is characterized as a reaction to an overwhelming sense of loss, real or imagined), and (3) *neurotic,* which is caused by a maladaptive personality.

In all three categories there are varying manifestations. They are all subject to differing intensity, duration, and quality. He states that the general rule is that mild depression of whatever kind, though agonizing, is usually overcome and routine living is quickly picked up.

But if the intensity of the depression is moderate or severe, the rebound is not quick and the situation requires serious attention. Since depression and anger are intimately intertwined there is an explosive powder keg lurking under the thin skin of daily life. If this frightening power goes awry it can drain a life of all joy or erupt in wife beating, child abuse, and perhaps even suicide in some individuals.

In the last analysis each individual suffering from depression will have to decide the severity of his own affliction and the steps to be taken. The intent of this book is not to offer professional medical advice but to indicate some basic elements involved in depression as it relates to spirituality, to one's search for God. This book is based on the assumption that anything having to do with the health or sickness of man's personality casts vital shadows upon his spirit as well. One is inseparably intertwined with the other. Mental health is not a totally other thing than spiritual health; they are not mutually exclusive but touch each other at many points. The ability to genuinely name and deal with both the light and darkness within us is absolutely essential to personality development *and* to spirituality.

1.

Depression: Cause and Cure

There is a profound scriptural theme concerning the concept of "name." Our own culture uses names as external tags, whereas the ancient Biblical tradition is that a name tells us what a thing is *in itself*. It tells us some of the essence of the reality named. Thinking along these lines, we must know a thing from the inside to correctly "name it." Thus to truly know a name is to have power over the named.

At this very moment there is a four-year-old girl lying in the hospital. Her hip joint is deteriorating. As terrible as this is, the greatest anguish is that no one knows why. There is as yet no name for the disease. The best specialists available have been consulted. All their tests have not revealed the name and thus the nature of the affliction. Unnamed, it cannot be treated.

This delightful, outgoing child has undergone a

radical personality change in the past few months. Such a ravaging sickness must indeed raise grave doubts in the child's mind about the goodness of life. "If this is 'life' how can it be embraced as good? How can anyone go out to meet and greet it?" If only they could find out what the problem is they might be able to do something and thus re-create some sunrise in her spirit. But there is no name.

Of course it works the other way too. Not only that which we fear needs to be named if we are ever to have any power over it but also that which we love and hunger to embrace. Not that we have to know the name to touch it. Frequently it is in love that names emerge. For when we love we see with an inner eye. That is the whole point with names — they tell us something of the inner reality of person or object.

Two little boys' faces come to mind. Like the girl in the hospital they are very young. Unlike her, they are surrounded neither by disease nor by a living family. At such a tender age they are very much on their own.

But there is another lady in their neighborhood who is like Santa Claus and sunshine all rolled into one. Apparently the little boys' mother told them not to bother the neighborhood. In the strange almost Biblical way that concepts arise in children's minds the Santa Claus lady became "the neighborhood." To them, that is her name.

How did this happen? When the boys would throw stones at her car or knock over garbage cans this lady would always stop and talk to them. But never in anger. She touched their faces and their hearts by her gentle words and hands.

The boys found their way to her house; and now each day, at least once, they come to the back door and shout their desperate plea, "Is the neighborhood home? Will she come out and talk to us?"

It's not everyone who can in themselves be a whole neighborhood to someone. The lady's name might be any of our traditional Western names: Mary, Susan, Ellen. But those names only distinguish her from other ladies, they don't tell a thing *about her*. The children however gave her a name that means something. "The neighborhood" truly says who she is to them.

Several events in Scripture pointedly offer this same insight. The creation account informs us that the man "made from dust" (Adam) was to name the animals. As man, he was higher than the animals; and his knowledge of their inner workings gave him power over them.

The ancient Jews were not allowed to pronounce the name of God. Anything else was unthinkable. To know a name was to have power over the reality; to name something — like "the neighborhood" — was to know it. But who can have power over God? Who but God could know God?

Thus the importance of naming realities. It doesn't take much reflection to realize how important it is to name things correctly. A misnamed reality becomes a tremendous danger. When we do this intentionally, we are playing a most dangerous game. We are saying that we do not want to know the truth. When we turn our back on truth we eliminate the possibility of ever getting better.

NAME IT CORRECTLY

If we have decided to hang on a cross (and we will even if we have not decided to) we should try to hang on the right one. Only the correct cross can bring us to the empty cave of the Resurrection. A few examples might help to clarify this point.

Not long ago on a rather complex series of speaking engagements in different parts of the country, I was scheduled to fly from San Francisco to New Orleans. From there I was to catch a specific flight to Atlanta. It had been a long flight from California after a long day. By the time I got to the Crescent City the last thing I wanted or needed was trouble. But there I was told the travel agency had scheduled me on a flight that no longer existed. I was stranded rather late at night knowing I had to start a workshop the next morning in another city.

Fortunately there was one last flight leaving New Orleans by another airline that night. I had only a two-hour wait.

At the time I really didn't care. I fully welcomed the two hours just to sit. There was no particular anger or resentment toward the agency. In fact I was pleased at this turn of events.

A week later I was scheduled to do a workshop for some 200 ladies at a neighboring school. I have no excuse for this, not one in the world — but I forgot. Many things were going on at the time, and I was out of my office doing something else. Upon my return my secretary informed me that the school principal had been calling every five minutes. All the ladies were there, the evening had been lined up for months; I just didn't show.

By the time I finally arrived, face red as war paint, it was too late. All I could do was feel terribly embarrassed, apologize, and go home.

The strange thing that happened however, and the point about naming things correctly, was the worse I felt about this embarrassing event, the more I wanted to call the travel agency in a fit of total anger and let them know how much they had inconvenienced me a week before. "That was no way to run a business, and what was wrong with them anyway!"

In truth of course, I wasn't angry at the travel agency. I was angry, embarrassed, disappointed in myself. If I had allowed myself to hang on the wrong cross, or misname it completely, not only would the real cause of the pain not have been touched but I would have hurt many innocent people. It is one thing to confront the enemy. It is quite another to know who the enemy is.

Even the ability to accurately name just what it was I did feel was critical. To be sure, I felt terrible. But why?

The acceptable "name" was that I let all those people down, that they had counted on me, that I had caused great inconvenience. All of which was true. But was it most deeply true? If that was as far as it went, would it have been enough to truly heal me in a way that also would be of benefit and growth?

Close friends helped me understand that there was a large element of pride involved here. It was a question of being able to forgive self and get on with living *humbly*. They brought up the point that if it had happened to someone else, one of the people I live with for example, I would have been quick to urge him to forgive himself, to point out that everyone makes mistakes, and that he should not take it harder than the people who were stood up. We are so quick to lay a lot of nice advice on someone else, but somehow we are so slow to apply it to ourselves. If we are going to hang on a cross, hang on the right one. Name it what it is.

There is a great temptation here to pick out a name that is acceptable. Many people may name pride as their basic living problem. It is "O.K." for people to be full of pride — so our culture teaches.

Often the real name — hiding behind the mask of pride — is fear. If a man rushes out and buys a car he can't afford because the neighbor has just gotten a new one, he may call it pride. Underneath however what often lurks is fear: If I don't get a comparably priced car, I may not look as good or think *I am* as good as he.

The same often is true of perfectionists. Our materialistic, perfectionistic society says that this is an acceptable fault. To be a perfectionist is a "cute" kind of character defect — one that is easily understood. But not many people want to live with it.

When the pain of being a perfectionist becomes so great that its victim seeks to do something about it, what often emerges is neurotic perfectionism. And that too is often fear — fear that if things aren't "in order," they will get away from me. Often there is a transference from an inability to keep the inner house of spirit in order, so I project it onto the outer world around me. I try to substitute one for the other.

We can't cure or resolve a living problem through relieving a symptom. Cures are brought about only when the cause is seen for what it is and dealt with in some creative way. The causes of the suffering in our life are the crosses. But these crosses can give way to glorious renewal of life — *if* they are first named and named accurately.

Take the matter of loneliness. There are millions of people in our alienated world who feel alone and are *sure* they know the reason. Because (a) no one is there to share with, (b) because no one would understand what they have to say anyway, (c) because no one has time to share, (d) because most people have enough problems of their own. (Perhaps you could add a few more.)

All of these are "names" and crosses. But are they the right names? Might not the real reason be that we won't give anyone else a chance? In fact there are people "out there" able and willing, perhaps begging to be let into the circle of our life. But as with all else there is a price tag — a fearful one. There is much rock that must be scraped away — painfully inch by inch — before new life can emerge. The price has names like risking vulnerability, being ready to surrender, showing a willingness to admit "I need you."

But too often we do not want to know those names, to admit them. For then we would be put in a place of having to make conscious decisions about them. It is far easier (and more lonely) to say "no one is there" than to say "I chose not to let anyone in." But in reality what is the true name of the problem?

Before applying this point of true naming to our basic theme of depression, I feel it important to say that healing is not solely dependent on deep self-analyzation and introspection. There is no need for every thought, word, and deed to be examined under a magnifying glass. We do not have to become neurotic about digging into our past, evaluating everything ever said or done to us. Healing is in the present, not just finding reasons for our brokenness from the past.

The point is that full human life demands self-honesty. Healing or getting better necessitates the operation of the "hermit" in our lives. We all need that attitude which would permit us to honestly see, if we can and as far as we can at this moment, to know what we are about. We need those moments of solitude that enable us to listen to and hear our own song being sung. Without such quiet moments we are strangers to ourselves and seem doomed to constantly inflict blind confusion and pain on those around us. To be sure we all have a "junk room" within. Original sin is one name for it. If we want to turn that room into an indoor garden, we must first know where it is. Then we must be willing to let others in so they too can see it. And once we discover that someone else can look upon it and see at least the possibility of flowers growing there, then the world somehow becomes sweeter.

Honesty and trust grow together. The more we gently, slowly learn to trust, the more confidence we have in being honest. In reverent love do names emerge. And they are the real names.

ANGER A CAUSE OF DEPRESSION

There is a name in our culture we are taught to dislike. We are taught that "good people" don't feel this way. That name is anger. Good people don't get angry.

But at least one major theory of depression claims that it is always associated with repressed anger. Anger that has been submerged, pushed under, misnamed. Anger we do not admit to and thus deal with in some inappropriate way.

But whenever we try to deal with something that has been misnamed, intentionally or not, it can never be healing or creative. (All the ranting and raving in the world at the travel-agency people would not have helped them, me, or the people I stood up at the neighboring school.)

Let us take a look at this thing called anger. At times we confuse creative anger with violent, ugly rage. Are those people who fly into uncontrolled rage dealing with their anger? Not true. Rage is the result of undealt-with anger. Like trying to cap a volcano we continue to push painful, anger-causing thoughts and events down inside us until there is no room for anything but an explosion. It is a ticking time bomb, and when the explosion occurs there is all heat and no light. This means no insight flows from it and frequently considerable pain befalls the individual and those around him. Dealing creatively with anger differs from attending to out-of-control rage.

It is not only a fascinating but extremely enriching meditation to take the thought of "anger" into your hermit's retreat and reflect upon it.

Recently I was able to attend a workshop on depression. Part of the program was a panel of three doctors and two psychiatrists. They cited startling statistics on the percentages of their patients who were in fact suffering from mild, modest, or severe depression — whether they were in touch with their depression or not. One thing became clear. Psychic stress will eventually lead to a bodily confrontation. Something in the body will break down. Again, it may well be only a symptom of what is really wrong. The doctors' insight was that many people were out of touch with their anger as well. Some of their examples might serve us well.

Depression was nearly always associated with a sense of loss. The loss might be through death; or it might concern loss in a material sense (for example, a home, a job, money) or a loss of self-image. Again they made the distinction between the necessary period of natural grief over a loss and that prolonged, paralyzing state of sickness known as depression. The point was emphatically made that depression is a general condition in which anger seems always to play a part.

One doctor cited that in his practice widows or widowers who suffer from depression can often be helped to understand that they were angry at the spouse who died. With enough help they can be led to verbalize some of these feelings of hostility. For example, they might say, "If only he would have taken better care of himself," or, "Now I'm left with this immense task of raising these children."

However this is a difficult task because we have been trained to think that it is unbecoming for a widow (or widower) to feel anger toward a loved one who is dead. How could you be angry at a dead spouse? And isn't it gross selfishness to even think about how hard it is going to be raising the kids when *he/she has died?*

And so what has been called the "slush fund" starts to build. The true name gets lost in the confusion and pain of the situation. It doesn't get dealt with, it is pushed under. You can be sure as bitter winter follows mellow fall, the depression fog will start to roll in. A heaviness starts to pull at the heart and the sun is less bright.

Sometimes, too, this unnamed anger is directed toward God. Obviously, this becomes a confusing problem for fervent Christians. We have always been told, and believe, that God is a good God. He is Father, "Abba." "It just isn't right to be angry at God. It might even be a sin!"

To prevent this, Christian tradition has built up a veritable storehouse of sayings to supposedly eliminate any thought of anger toward God. "It is God's will." "Good will come out of it." "He knows best."

All of these sayings are basically true. But that isn't the point. The point is that unnamed anger creates serious problems — one of which is severe depression. So it becomes important to acknowledge whatever it is you feel; for then you can deal with it and can rob it of its power to destroy. Consciousness is the light of the soul.

No matter how good a Christian you are, if you are angry at God, it is vital that you allow yourself to know what you feel. As one saying puts it, "The only way out is through." We can't get out of our anger by trying to go around it. We must look at it, acknowledge it, embrace it.

The tragic thing that happens to Christians who are not able (willing) to admit their possible hostile feelings toward God is that they continue to exteriorly worship their loving God. The same prayers are said. The same religious practices are followed. But slowly, surely, the feeling evaporates. The final refuge, who was God, begins to fade away. The warmth that could not be cooled ceases to warm them.

The next step is that they are plagued with doubts about loss of faith. In a genuine agony they wonder why God has taken himself away from them. "What have they done? Where are they to turn now?"

But God hasn't gone anywhere. He doesn't love less. What has happened is that this unnamed hostility has cast its shadow between the seeking soul and the Sun. Unnamed, it is unseen.

It has often been my privilege to witness a person working through these hostile feelings. What a joy to see this person once again experiencing the warmth of the saving Lord flowing back into his soul. Then those sayings that were platitudes take on a new meaning. Now they have become expressions of faith. They have stood the test of courage to face what is, and through that courage found the joy of inner knowledge.

Shortly after this workshop on depression and anger I visited a friend in the hospital. He was a late middle-aged widower suffering from varied physical ailments, but mental turmoil seemed to be his main problem. He was a staunch Catholic and had been a widower for well over a decade.

We sat and talked for quite some time. With these new thoughts in mind, I asked him point-blank if he was angry about anything. He assured me he was not. It was not right to be angry. (To him, anger meant rage.) Besides, he had his God, didn't he? What else did anyone need?

This man, let us call him Paul (for like many of us he was not totally unlike Saul on his horse needing a good bolt of lightning to rearrange his head), truly is a good man who seeks the Lord. He is open to talk and discussion. And at this given time he was most ready for any help he could get. Paul was suffering great mental and physical turmoil.

We talked about anger.

Paul had been married for 17 unhappy years. Slowly he began to admit that just maybe he was somewhat angry over those difficult years. Angry at his wife, angry at society, angry at his family who seemed to think it was good he got married.

The death of his wife had left him with considerable property. The land has now become low-rent housing land. Over the past few years there has been immense trouble with threats and violence.

In responding to this he acted the way he thought a good Christian should act: he prayed for these people — even when they threatened to burn his house down and shoot him. This was no excuse for anger but rather a great cause for prayer.

But there in that dark room at the late night hour he admitted that there might be some justification for the thought he could be just a tiny bit angry at them. Before I left he came around on this point to admit he was absolutely furious.

In addition, he had just been swindled out of a very large sum of money by a supposed "friend." And up till this point the treatment of this tragedy was to pray for the man who betrayed him. He claimed there was no anger or resentment — just surprise that it could happen.

But again, after talking a long time, he came around to admitting that he was indeed angry at this fellow and deeply hurt. But his greatest anger was at himself for allowing himself to get in this position in the first place. After that admission the floodgates opened. He spoke about how much of a fool he felt himself to be — all the things he had done (driving to the bank with this person, drawing up the checks, signing them and handing them over). He could remember each step, detail after detail.

One of the physical ailments Paul suffered was a "burning, ball-like sensation that sat at the top of his stomach." After our several hours' talk he mentioned that it seemed to be gone, at least for the moment.

Anyone who has ever been in much contact with minority groups of any kind is in fact often staring at the face of anger; and often, what he sees is either suppressed or expressed violent rage. One such minority group are divorced people. Divorcees and divorcés are people who are alone in a unique manner. Of course, everyone is alone in a sense, but we are not all alone in the same way. There is even a very real difference, physical and mental and even cultural, between a divorcee or divorcé and a widow or widower.

Not long ago a group of divorced people got together for a discussion. These thoughts and feelings emerged:

When you are alone, Saturday nights and holidays are the worst times of all. They emphasize your aloneness. You feel so *sure* everyone else in the world is out having a good time with someone else, sharing love, being together. Feelings erupt. Feelings like loneliness, self-pity, fear, etc. But seldom did anger become consciously identified. It was more just a general feeling of unrest, agitation, sorrow.

But then one man in the group shared this situation. He had recently gone to a picnic. Being a divorced man, he was alone. But since he had been genuinely trying to deal with his living problems, he was able to go to this picnic with his friends and not be angry. Before confronting his anger he would not have had a good time, been nagged by this vague, general feeling of hostility and not actually known what was going on. But he really liked all these people. They truly were his friends and would not do a thing to hurt him. Yet he would have been angry at them whether he knew it or not. But no more. He had a wonderful time. He could be there, see all these couples together, know that they all went home with each other even if their marriages were far from perfect.

What would have been going on before he got in touch with his anger was all these familiar questions like "Why me?" "What did I ever do to deserve this?" "Why did my marriage have to go on the rocks?" He said the questions were more feelings than verbalized questions — and that was much of his problem, they were *not* verbalized. They were too vague and pushed under to even know enough about them to put a word to them. But being unnamed didn't mean they were powerless. Quite the opposite. They become all the more powerful when unnamed. The only thing more frightening than being honest is being dishonest, for then you give over your life into the uncontrolled power of that which you will not face.

So minority groups are frequently angry, whether they know it or not. In a real sense, however, who is not a member of a minority? Each minority has about it that which can easily create anger and this anger then becomes either stumbling block or stepping stone. Take, for example, being a woman.

There is much in our culture that creates categories of thought and being which are grossly unfair to women. Unfair because they are counter-productive to human growth which leads to happiness. This is not to say the same is not true for men. But it is also very true for women.

If the walls of any priest's parlor, psychiatrist's office or doctor's clinic could talk, what stories they would tell of the increasing mental stress due to anger when the consciousness level of woman's role begins to rise. And I mean black, blue, rageful anger. Often it is pushed under and burns with a slow fuse, but it is burning and it will take its toll in one way or another.

There is a night club not far from my office. It sits on a busy highway. In front of the club is a large sign advertising a wet T-shirt contest, with the lucky winner being given $100.

There is also a good friend of mine whose consciousness level has risen to the point where she knows the difference between being used creatively or as a plaything. She is a beautiful woman with two absolutely beautiful teen-age daughters.

Every time I happen to be with her and pass that sign her eyes narrow and I can just see the pot start to boil. She has been used and used badly. She knows the indignity of it all, where it can lead in terms of loss of self-respect and self-acceptance. She hates that whole cultural trap that would hold women up as amusement or toys; she violently hates it for herself but perhaps even more so for her lovely daughters.

The wonderful thing about this woman is that she knows she hates it and feels perfectly justified in being very angry at it. There is an old saying that goes "If someone calls you a horse long enough, pretty soon you will start looking for a saddle." But she now knows enough to be able to hear all the subtle ways this can be said. You cannot help hearing it, but you can help accepting it. She isn't buying any more.

The point again is she *knows* she isn't. This named, faced anger no longer has power to add heaviness to her heart. Her legitimate anger does not cause her to become depressed. Our natural reaction to stress and strain is the "fight or flight" syndrome. We try to do something about the stress either by fighting it in some way or running from it. Depression comes when we stop fighting or running. We just sit down and allow ourselves to be eaten alive by the affliction. That is why depression is exemplified by apathy, a do-nothing attitude. We just don't have the energy or ambition to do anything. We are tired, worn out.

Unnamed anger — which is not the simple, simplistic core of depression, but does seem to be a central piece — is a heavy weight to carry around. Enough of it will make us want to stop, and in fact actually do so. Then we are easy prey for the wolves.

The fact that this woman can be angry at that sign, even if she cannot do anything about it (but she has some grand ideas on that score), keeps her at least one step ahead of the wolves.

As strange as it may seem, beautiful women are at a distinct disadvantage in our culture. For one thing, exterior beauty (along with youth) has been molded into a god which the vast majority worship with no question or thought. The trouble is, of course, that no one can ever be beautiful enough. If that could happen, how would all the beauty aids be sold?

The terrible tendency of several sick cultural concepts is to consider beautiful women merely as ornaments. They are exhibited on certain occasions by their husbands. Beauty becomes a possession to be had like land or stocks. On special occasions it is proper to show off what you "have." Even if this is not consciously done, the prevailing attitude is still influencing all.

The obvious problem here is that exterior beauty is being substituted for person. As one lovely lady told me, "I don't want to be a fragile china doll stuck up on a shelf. I want to be a person with whom my husband will share himself. I want to be a partner, not a possession."

"Sterile" is a word often used in this context. What good is it to be beautiful on the outside if you feel sterile on the inside? China dolls are lovely to look at but you never know them from inside. That knowledge is only arrived at when person meets person, when respect and love replace attitudes of use and abuse, when surrender melts into another surrender.

When all of these negative categories — being beautiful for the sake of beauty, being an ornament, being used — get shoved down long enough rage develops. It may express itself in many different forms; but it is there, under the layers of rock. And as long as that rage boils away, things can't ever be right. Or as right as they could be.

What is not named has unlimited power to cause us trouble. That unnamed power rumbling about in our spirit-temple demands ever increasing amounts of energy to keep it submerged, hidden. Very seldom does anything change except by conscious decision. And so as the years and months go by more and more gets pushed under and the rage grows deeper. Energy that could be spent embracing joyful life is spent preventing life from eating us alive. We construct endless escapes — more prayer, harder work, more activity — to escape our general unrest. Somehow it doesn't work. Something is still lacking.

Perhaps, just as a suggestion, anger is a name we should think about. Anger before it becomes rage, rage before it finally drags us down to where we just stop and, sitting down, surrender ourselves to the wolves.

IMPORTANCE OF SELF-ESTEEM

We sit down or withdraw from the arena of life when we figure we have no sword with which to fight. We lose hope when there are no longer any options open to us, or at least any we can see. As long as we retain our ability to make any decisions at all about our course of life we also retain our freedom. Freedom is the ability to decide. Not just that we say yes or no, but that we can say one *or* the other.

The obvious central core to this is self-esteem. A good self-image is vital to creative life. If you truly think you are a horse or cow, why not run for the saddle or yoke? And in fact you will. There is a close relationship between loss of self-esteem (a good self-image) and anger. One feeds the other.

If it is true that possibly there is a residue or reservoir of anger boiling inside of us, then why not face it? Simple *lack of knowledge* is one reason. Perhaps we have no idea of some of the anger that is in us. We might be well aware of some of the manifestations of this repressed anger but possibly have no hint of where these negative expressions originate.

In that case some surrendering prayer and honest dialogue with others is in order.

Perhaps another reason might well be our *fear*. We are subtle creatures and somehow decide many issues without consciously being aware of it. For every wound of anger there is an option: we can face what is bothering us. But if that is done there might well be some further decisions that must be made. Decisions we would rather not make. And so on some deep level we decide not to see. We choose blindness.

It immediately becomes obvious what this does to self-esteem however. Again on some deeper than conscious level we know we are cheating ourselves. We know we are allowing someone else to ruin our happiness and steal our serenity. We know it and allow it, thus eventually losing all respect for ourselves.

One result that faced-anger often brings in its wake is the need for a confrontation of some kind. This need not be violent, ugly, or bloody. It might simply be the courage to say, "I don't understand this, I mean, why you did it. It bothered me though." It might well be a self-confrontation — like the woman who sees the sign advertising the T-shirt contest — which admits that we don't like this action or category of thought. If at work or at home things are intolerable, it might be a first step to admit that it is in fact intolerable. Who knows where it goes from there? But that of course is just the point. It might well lead to something else, other decisions. This road of honesty is not a freeway. Freedom takes its toll.

And yet the other way is far from free either. Both ways hurt. The only question is what we will buy with our pain. One is a death-to-death process. The other becomes a death-to-life. In both there is a death. Only in one is there a life.

To live under a galling situation and accept it, even to the point of not allowing ourselves to admit that it is galling, is emotional suicide. What gets sacrificed at the altar of peace-at-any-price is self-esteem. The murder weapon is fear.

The existential psychologists today speak a great deal about man's "broken will." They say that in our supermechanized world we have lost the sense of our own destiny. We have too much surrendered to the machine. Things get too big, too complex. We lose touch with those decisions that affect and in fact control our lives. We give up the right to make decisions about who we shall be. In a word, we become power-less. Apathy and mediocrity become the norms to such an extent that anyone who would speak a word otherwise becomes a threat. So much so that if the word is potent enough, in simple truth the singer of that song must be silenced. Prophets get killed. The process is as old as man.

But people cannot lie down and die on the altar of broken wills unless they first lose all sense of their own power. And the source of that sense of power is a grand and glorious proclamation that I *am me.*

That wonderful, unique sense of self-worth is the opposite of apathy. The sense of self-worth is precisely what apathy undermines. The most noble figures of our human, national, or personal history are those who taught us in word and deed that "Yes, I can. I am me and yes, I can." From that vital lesson we learn "and so can I." John Neihardt, in one of his exhilarating books about the first Americans, says that life is at its fullness when man has climbed the mountain and seen the great vision. Although that climb is shot through with humility and the sense of something being born larger than self, there is still the unshakable sense that I am me and I shall see the vision!

The "sitting down" that precedes depression includes the surrender of my own vision of who I am. Once this happens no light can stream from the darkened eye.

Any learned, cultured person who has ever written on the rise and fall of civilizations, the memorable steps of the ascent of man, always speaks of those peak moments in a society's existence when it was aflame with self-confidence. Creativity demands self-confidence. It is the statement that here, in this moment, I am the willing servant of the creative Power greater than myself. I am a brush in the hand of God.

As true as this is of civilizations it is also true of individuals. Everyone is called upon to live a creative life. Life cannot be joyful or full without creativity which proclaims in writing a letter, picking the color of your room, or choosing the kind of music you like — This is me. I am here.

Self-esteem is the eye from which this light streams. To lose self-esteem is to surrender to apathy: we forget our own names, who we are, and who we could be. We give up being the architects of our own world.

How early do we start learning who we are? When do we first learn that "I am not good enough"? When do we first start to suspect that we are not making the grade? Who first starts laying the groundwork of categories that we may well live in the rest of our lives?

The insights of competent specialists tell us that we face these questions when we are very young. And so the basic fuel for our anger may well be planted in us during the first weeks or months of life. Not by accident do we become the persons we are. If we truly knew the dispositions and environment of others, our exclamation would not be "How could they be that way?" but "How could they be any other way?"

I am thinking of several of our pre-teens and teen-agers. It is certainly true that self-doubt and self-discovery are synonymous with that state of life. That is the business at hand for them. But there is something else naggingly true about them and almost every one of their peers, to say nothing of the adults around them. They seem not to like themselves too well. They are full of doubts about their own power.

One little girl of about ten, breathtakingly beautiful, thinks she is ugly. Her legs, to her, look funny. A teen-ager who is just an excellent baseball player would rather be boiled in oil than admit it. Compliments become absolute torture. Warm, lovely moments when a friend, relative — whoever — simply wants to say "I am glad you are in my world, you beautify it, you mean a great deal to me" become agonizing experiences. That they have any gift to give and that anyone would want the gift if they had it in the first place has made them lose confidence in themselves.

Thus we do encounter the dragons of life without a sword. Or better yet, we pass the flowers of life without eyes to see their beauty or noses to smell their fragrance. We face the daily routine from a position of weakness: I have little and am little and may well not make the struggle at all. We submit to this rather than greet life from a stance of strength: The world is full of beauty and I have my own unique gift to share with others and be enriched by their loveliness as well.

To more than a few these concepts are shrugged off as luxury. "They are icing on the cake when I am concerned with finding just a bit of hard bread. Nice but not important."

The opposite is true. Self-esteem is absolutely necessary for a full life. There is scarcely any gift more important for parents to communicate to their children than the knowledge that they are something special. And every moment and event of life is something special. It has been truly said the greatest gift parents can give their children is the knowledge that as spouses they love one another. But look at all that is involved if this is to happen.

To accept the fact that you are loved automatically involves accepting that you are worth loving. And this indeed may well be the prime obstacle to more loving relationships. So often we feel we aren't worthy of being loved, to be graced by anyone else's gift of self. We will give till there is nothing left to give; yet we refuse to give the greatest gift, which is accepting the love of another.

It is impossible to lead anyone where we have not been ourselves. We can walk into the unknown, trustingly, with another. But we cannot lead where we have not been. We cannot invite others to a freedom we have never known.

If we are involved in the deadly process of not being in touch with our feelings — in this particular case, anger — then it probably will also be true that depression, technical or general, will soon be upon us. As the unnamed wolves gradually pull us down we slow up and give up. Apathy takes over. Self-esteem drains away. Creativity becomes a luxury we cannot muster. Just as with the death of all great civilizations we witness the loss of self-confidence, the closing of the door to communion with the gods, so too we lose our personal creative powers when we lack self-confidence.

It is the twilight before the awful darkness. But the question is, must it be that way?

NECESSITY OF PERSONAL RESPONSIBILITY

A key healing element in the psychiatrists' response to the condition of the broken will is responsibility. They emphasize the necessity of taking our stand against the world as opposed to being done unto by the world. We do have a responsibility to ourselves not to surrender our power of choice.

Anger, from which grows depression, must be countered. Alone it simply grows to rage and degenerates into violence. If the junk room is to become an indoor garden, there is need for another to be allowed within our walls.

So often, however, we say there is no one we can trust. For all kinds of reasons we conclude that no one loves us. But is that the truth? Might it not simply be a matter of responsibility on our part to seek until there is someone who can be trusted within?

We cannot grow without stretching. And that stretching also is a matter of our own responsibility. There are decisions that can be made regarding our own slavery, our own layers of rock. No one ever said it is or would be easy, but that isn't the same as saying it isn't possible.

A favorite trick of many people in avoiding responsibility for their own growth is to blame it on the past. If they can do that successfully enough, they can relinquish any responsibility for the present and future.

For example, listen sometime to people explaining why they have dropped out of the Church. Often, their reasons go back to some nun who was mean to them, a priest who chased them out of the sacristy, a Church teaching (actually, a custom) that has been abandoned. These are all convenient ways of avoiding duty to self.

Who hasn't run into cranky priests and Sisters? But then who hasn't run into cranky bus drivers, store clerks, or other unhappy people? Yet we keep riding the bus and going to the store. These people don't really threaten our comfort zone.

But comfort zones are also tender zones. Anyone who has been pushed to the wall by some situation and simply *had* to confront a comfort zone knows well the price that must be paid. Honesty and trust may well be the two most painful prizes we can win. Oh, but the sweetness when they have been won!

Again, any priest's counseling room or any room where people pour out their sorrows could tell the heartrending agony of facing the fact of learning to trust. Either that or go under. "The pain simply has grown too great. Yes, even that situation or truth I simply *knew* I could tell no one. Or my difficulties in marriage, my loneliness, my feelings of being used or passed over when merit badges of some kind were given out. Those hidden truths that lead to rage — even those. In fact, especially those. For these are the weights that are dragging me down."

Obviously, such hesitation arises from the fear of what will happen if anyone knew! "If I shared with them these *weak* feelings, surely they would leave me all alone. They would throw me away like a used paper cup. And that is what I fear above all: rejection. If I were not afraid of that, there would be no problem in trusting."

But there is a problem. Shattered self-esteem cannot stand rejection. So abhorrent is it that if possible many of us would willingly chose exile from the communion of others rather than share. We would rather say most anything but "Help me."

And yet it doesn't have to be that way. If we can come to the point where we take responsibility for our own lives, they can become better, brighter, more full of joy. But it is our choice. We can learn to share with others who can handle that great privilege and gift.

With true insight, Dr. Karl Jung years ago observed that what is most personal to us is also most universal to all men. It is precisely those thoughts we bury the deepest that are the most common to all, those feelings which we are so *sure* no one else has ever felt that are felt by the majority. We are so much alike in our pain, in our need for one another, in our grace-filled ability to be "answer" for one another.

QUESTION OF NATIONAL SURVIVAL

Lord Kenneth Clark is surely one of the foremost authorities on culture and civilization in the world today. Repeatedly in his classic book *Civilization* he makes the point that nations and societies are but collections of individuals. It is the collective health and positive attitudes of the people that make up the very innards of the nation.

To the degree that individuals of a culture fear introspection and honesty, so in like manner will the country. As an individual forsakes the primacy of his own decision-making power concerning his destiny and begins to call on outer forces for protection, so does the national consciousness. When individuals fail to believe in themselves they cry out for Big Brother to come and save them.

Many, of course, have a neurotic fear of government. This fear may well be justified. But when individuals lose their confidence, anonymous leadership groups almost automatically take over.

The problem lies not so much with Big Government as with a lack of the Big Individual.

What is being said here is that what is important for individuals — the power to decide about their own lives — is essential for the national life as well. Only healthy people can possibly make a healthy country. The very qualities of a healthy person also exemplify a healthy culture, society, and nation.

These telling signs of a growing culture — heroic energy, strength of will and intellect, a drive for excellence, the visual expressions of the elegant ideals embraced by that society, etc. — are always couched in the atmosphere of confidence. Without confidence a society just can't grow or maintain itself.

We can learn many lessons about confidence and survival from the history of other nations. There was nothing the ancient Greeks, for example, thought they couldn't do. And there was little they didn't do. We not only draw from them the intellectual concept of democracy and personal freedom but even the underpinnings of that concept: the belief in the dignity of individual man. We take that so much for granted today — at least in the abstract — that it is nearly impossible for us to understand the radical sound it must have had in that far away time of kings, despots, and the universal belief that magic and the supernatural whim of the gods ruled men's lives.

Edith Hamilton, one of the great scholars of Greek culture, sadly remarks that scarcely a generation after the incredibly heroic battles of Marathon, Thermopylae, and Salamis, the Greek culture could no longer inspire such feats. Their culture was on the wane. The people had lost the ideals, the energy, and confidence to be larger than life. They accepted the role of mediocrity and surrendered the giant that was in them.

One feeds into the other to be sure, but great works of art or other expressions of a healthy society are not just the products of a gifted few. They are the products of the society. To a large extent it is the prevailing attitude of the culture that dictates who and what we shall be. When courage, confidence, the will to go on cease to be accepted norms of existence, it is but a matter of time before the culture exhausts itself.

Leon Battista Alberti was one of the early statesmen of that marvelous time in Western history called the Renaissance. It was a time of such great joy and exuberant energy. Once when speaking of man, he said what may sound foolish to us: "To you is given a body more graceful than other animals . . . to you, wit, reason, memory like an immortal god." But the people of 14th-century Florence believed it. And from that belief and confidence flowed a garden of history.

André Malraux, the one-time director of the great Art Institute in France — while commenting on the 500th anniversary of Michelangelo — said that we shall not have another man like him. His reason: We no longer believe in man.

So it is not just a happy thought that people get in touch with their feelings, that anger and hostility become named, that self-esteem be accepted as a central responsibility of life. It is absolutely vital not only to the people who suffer from depression, which always includes a loss of confidence, but it is essential to the continued life of any nation as well.

Keeping these thoughts in mind, we ask what prayer has to do with all of this? Understood properly, prayer can work wonders for the depressed. But this is the topic of our next chapter.

2.

What Prayer Can Do

Every school child knows the difference between a noun and an adjective. Nouns name different objects. They designate separate realities. They keep things apart.

Adjectives indicate separate qualities of the same thing. They are like windows in the same house that allow us to see the same dwelling from many different vantage points. Adjectives allow us to know an object with greater scope, with more insight.

For a long time now we have seen spirituality and psychology as nouns. We have acted as if they were totally different — almost as though they were enemies. (Science and religion have been treated in much the same way down through the ages.) But suppose we view them not as nouns but as adjectives allowing us access from differing doors to the same reality, which in this case is man — man struggling to live as whole and holy a life as possible.

Part of the immense tragedy of ruling out any discipline that can tell us more about the inner workings of man with the simple heading of "Secular" is that it leaves our spirituality lacking. And far more serious, it may well leave it erroneous and thus tremendously dangerous. More than a decade ago the Council Fathers of Vatican II pointed out the decided interdependence of the sacred and the secular, the Church and the world, theology and psychology.

Sane, whole, holy living is the issue at hand. And man is the only creature capable of sanity or insanity, of holiness or accepted sin. Who we are, our manner of life, the direction we are going — these are the points in question. Dogmas or theories do not end up in mental wards or living, creative relationships: people do.

Prayer does have much to do with depression and unnamed anger. Prayer is a word from the realm of spirituality; depression suggests the field of psychology. Yet both are, or can be seen as, adjectives speaking about the common noun: man. But I warn you that prayer used in this context might not be exactly what is commonly understood as prayer. At the very outset of this chapter I would like to make a distinction concerning prayer. Then will follow an application of this distinction.

Let us look at prayer under the aspect of what we might call the prayer of the "outer embrace" and the prayer of the "inner search."

OUTER EMBRACE

What I draw attention to here is that aspect of prayer which is purely for the glory of God: the prayer of adoration. It is the lifting up of the heart to God, no matter where we are physically or mentally, to acknowledge that he is the All, the Real, the Universal, the Word behind all words and the Light illuminating every light.

All prayer has a flavor of this; for God is not only greater than man, he is totally other. He is not only different in degree but in kind. Our prayers to God are not like our pleas to a powerful friend, a president, or a general. God is not a president or a general. He is a friend who happens to be our Father.

When we lift our minds to God and dare to call him "Abba" as Jesus has taught us, it is different than even calling the most loving of all fathers "daddy." For as much as all loving fathers are a reflection of *the* loving Father shown us by Christ, they are not God.

Rabbi Heschel points out in a lovely and loving way that prayer begins where words end. We enter the domain of prayer when we arrive at that point where there just are no words to express what is rising in our hearts. Finally we stand in the temple where we know in our hearts that "I must decrease, he must increase." We are in the realm of "this is greater than I." "It is not so much that we want to pray," says the Rabbi, "but that God wants us to pray to him."

Thinking and reflecting on that point alone is enough to create a near endless desire to utter the prayer of outer embrace.

INNER SEARCH

Obviously, then, there is no quarrel with this outgoing prayer to God, this light of ours we cast out into the Infinite to "see" and grasp what we can. But that precisely is the essence of the prayer of the inner search! All too often this essence is lost in prayer manuals; all too often it is forgotten when we think of prayer. With what light *do* we seek God? With what depth do we receive him? With what capacity do we love?

All praying is not necessarily prayer. Praying is what flows from the attitude of prayer. But what do we believe about prayer? Father Henri Nouwen has written about prayer in a beautifully poetical book, *With Open Hands*. That phrase in itself speaks well of the attitude of prayer. Open hands are symbolic of open hearts. Open hearts are symbolic of open lives. An open life is one that is willing to engage in the inner search, to find those hidden, locked, unnamed doors and see what can be done about opening them and thus allowing the Light who is light to enter and dwell.

Father Nouwen uses the word picture of a person tightly holding random coins in his/her hand. The fist is clenched. Nothing can come in or go out. Nothing can be bought with the coins thus held. In a word, the attitude of the one clutching the coins renders them useless.

If only the hand could be coaxed open, freedom might be found: freedom to be unafraid of whatever it is that caused the hand to fold tightly over in the first place; freedom that would allow one to face what is there and find, hopefully, it is not quite so fearful after all; freedom to take what is held so tightly and transform it into something even better.

Many of us are victims of such slavery. We ignore the fact that our hand is a fist. The reasons are complex and strong, so we try to make it disappear by nonattention. The only trouble is this never works.

Ignoring a stomach ulcer — which stress, anger, and depression often cause — is a guarantee to make it get worse. It doesn't just go away.

As much as we would have it otherwise, the little saying "the only way out is through" is terribly true.

In how many ways do we try to go around? I might become furious at the travel agency for routing me on a nonexistent flight rather than admit I was angry at myself for forgetting my speaking engagement. But how does that help? It doesn't heal my anger or negative feelings because it wasn't the "through" that was wrong.

My friend at the picnic could have allowed himself to fall into a deep rage because he was alone and the others were family groups. He could have returned home with a thousand justified reasons why they were "laughing at him." Very easily he could have continued to clutch those coins in his hand and refused ever to attend another picnic.

The only way out is through. That wasn't his problem at all. No one was laughing at him. In fact, not everyone there was a member of a family group — not even the married people. How many of us not willing to pray the prayer of the inner search — to go through — continue to make others the enemy when in fact the only enemy is our clenched hand?

The prayer of the inner search demands a willingness to seek out who it is that is praying in the first place. It concerns itself not so much with the magnificence of the universe as with the candlepower of the telescope viewing it. It pertains not so much to the brilliance of the sun at noon as to the purity of the window the light is to pass through. The way to get light through a dirty window is not to turn on an artificial light inside but to clean the window.

When our attitude of prayer does not include that dimension which would take us into ourselves — into the difficult but so vitally important phase of turning our fist into an open, loving hand — we may well be in trouble. And so might those around us. Not to see who we are and are becoming and not to know even the location of our locked doors shows a willingness not to surrender our tightly clenched fist. How can God fill the depth in us if there is no depth to fill?

ANGER AND PRAYER

Is anger, named or unnamed, a psychological or spiritual problem? Does it have any bearing on faith, religion, and God? Is there any connection between prayer and depression either in becoming healed or slipping into further degradation?

Obviously I think there is. I ask you to simply reflect with me and see if you can identify with any of what I will share with you.

There are those ''religious'' people among us, perhaps sincere to the core, who yet are always in the posture of attack. Their whole life seems to shout out, "Beware, the enemy is at hand." Tragically, they have no time for an open hand to lovingly stroke a child's face or pick a flower. Theirs is always the fist. They are always ready to strike out, ready to "defend the Church against attack."

Anger necessarily musters an enemy. It is a fight reflex. But to fight is to fight against someone. And if we're not too sure just who the genuine enemy is, we will fight anyone or anything. The more power we give over to our unnamed anger, the larger becomes whatever or whomever we designate as "enemy." If the clenched fist becomes total, then the whole world is the enemy.

It doesn't take much insight to see how this is projected onto religion. It's never admitted toward God, of course. If that were admitted then we have a convincing reason to leave it all behind. No, God stays on his throne; "they" are the ones we must fight. It can be nuns or ex-nuns. Priests or ex-priests. It can be those extraordinary ministers of the Eucharist, or the pastor for not letting anyone be such a minister. And of course a natural enemy is to divide the Church up into old and new. It really doesn't matter which. Either one can as easily become the enemy, the target of hot anger.

This isn't to say that any movement, segment of society, or path of spirituality might well have something to get angry about. That isn't the point. What we are speaking of here is the continual *state* of defend/attack. The felt need to always be in a fighting pose is saying something far more about the gladiator than about the issue at hand.

There is that about the Gospel message of Christ that bespeaks the open hand. To follow in the way of Jesus and the genuine attitude of prayer is to be on the path of serenity, companionship, sympathy. If those marks are missing, if there is not the spirit of hospitality in one's life, then it might well be that a huge, clenched fist is blocking the spirit. And that fist possibly is anger.

Prayer then becomes not just a concern of spirituality but relates also to the psychology of man. And anger can be a major issue in both. Prayer must lead man to himself; it must help in getting man in touch with himself so he can recognize the fist wherever and whatever it might be. Praying that flows from this attitude of prayer always lets in the light.

APATHY AND PRAYER

It might happen that the object of anger is not determined. It remains a kind of feeling that settles into a vague, general sense of hopelessness. This also becomes a familiar posture easily recognizable today in religion and life. We have said that depression descends when we give up either the fight or the flight. When we no longer feel we can do anything about anything, apathy is present.

No, I'm not saying all apathy has its roots in untouched anger. Rollo May has insightfully said that powerlessness is the sense of having no control over our lives. It is loss of the sense of the ability to choose. When this happens what else is there to do but sit down and be eaten by the wolf?

Violence, he says, is a direct result of powerlessness. But that is the violent rage spoken of earlier which is not a creative dealing with anger.

Apathy indicates a lack of leadership, which in turn demands a fullness of enthusiasm. How wonderful it is to run into someone full of enthusiasm, someone who truly believes in something, who is willing to breathe life into a creed or concept. Even if we ourselves might not totally or at all agree with the creed, it is indeed refreshing to brush up against someone like that in this time when bumper stickers read, "Tomorrow called off for lack of interest."

Coming from the Greek word meaning "in God," enthusiasm surely relates to the world of spirituality and religion. Factors that are detrimental to enthusiasm definitely are spiritual considerations. Therefore, prayer which gets us in touch with ourselves so that apathy can be countered or avoided altogether is of prime importance in our day. Prayer of the inner search is the kind that allows creative leaders to rise in our midst.

There is a world-wide absence of leadership today. This lack certainly extends to the Church. And leadership, just as the "enemy syndrome," is more than a psychological consideration.

Such wonderful things could be, and are, going on in the contemporary realm of religion. It is a time of getting together, of taking down walls, a time of stupendous opportunities for clearing the mind's windows so that the light of God may enter our hearts and world. But there is always the need for leadership in this area. Apathy sabotages the effort; therefore its causes must be seen and dealt with. "It won't work," "It can't be done," "Things like that can't happen." Leadership is precisely that soaring confidence which sees a different vision and leads us where we have not been before. In the realm of love, community, God-with-us — yes, it can be done. It has been done, done by Christ long ago. The problem is not with the power to do it but with the psychological freedom to accept that power of the Spirit.

Leadership is a matter of energy. But how can there be the energy to do or dare anything if copious effort is expanded in fighting the enemy "out there" or repressing the anger inside? In how many meetings have great ideas been stifled and eventually killed by lack of enthusiasm and energy? There just wasn't the confidence to carry on.

Of course that was never named. Rather, "tradition," "new is good" or "old is the only way," "the people aren't ready for it," "the Pope won't like it" are some of the reasons used.

On a more personal level than official Church structure, think of all the reasons we can manufacture for avoiding the occasions of our own spiritual growth. It might be any of many opportunities, making a retreat, reading a book, joining a prayer group, entering into discussion with others, attending a seminar. Just by saying one positive thing to one person can often make the difference. Even if it is a critical word it becomes positive because it was said rather than sat on.

Reasons might be, "It sounds dull," "I'm too dumb," "I'm too busy," "They are too dumb." But is any of these the right reason? It might well be that we are too tired or afraid or insecure. It might well be that apathy has such a hold that there really isn't much interest. We might keep right on praying; but which attitude of prayer have we adopted? Is it the prayer of inner search, the prayer of getting in touch with ourselves in order to find out who we are and who we want to be? If so, eventually we will without doubt be led to that locked door behind which are the clanking and rattling of slavery's chains. We will be led to look at the end of our own arm where the coins of faith are tightly clenched in a fist of suppression. Whether we overcome our apathy is very much a question of the meaning of prayer.

Leadership cannot very well be experienced on a group level till it at least is begun to be exercised on the personal level. In a very real sense we must be our own leaders. How shall we ever lead anyone else to increased freedom and the world of the open-handed touch rather than the fisted blow if we have not been willing to go there ourselves?

Religion is notorious for its exclusivity. "We belong, you don't." "We are saved, you are not." "We are good, you are bad." "There is but one way, ours." "If you are not following our way, you simply do not exist."

This is not to deny the validity of Christ's proclamation that "only he who comes to me will find the Father" and other such words. It does deny, however, the attitude that we are an exclusive, superior group set apart and the need to project such an attitude.

The fist cannot become clenched until the mind does. A mind that is not open to learn, to find the God above God, to find a way yet more excellent is simply not open to the words of God being spoken constantly throughout the day. It was such hardness of heart that froze up the Pharisees' minds and allowed them to crucify the Light. How many victims of "holiness" must our history parade before us till we learn that Jesus is found in the attitude of servant and guest? He was born in a humble stable not a fortified castle.

There is much written today about the concept of the God above God — the thought being that God is greater than any concept about God. He is always more than we can imagine him to be, his love deeper than our capacity to understand. Therefore our vocation as God-seeking people is always to search for the God above our present concept of God. Wherever we are now with God we can be further; for his capacity is infinite and we are capable of growth.

Such growth however demands an attitude of courage which is intimately entwined with praying and will be considered later. I only mention it here to stress the point at which apathy and enthusiasm part ways. Apathy, from whatever cause, becomes consummately satisfied with the God now grasped. It seeks no more. It expends only the energy to defend what is.

Enthusiasm on the other hand has no such restraints. It willingly admits the greatness of God, the need for further capacity to know him. Enthusiasm constantly thirsts for the God above God, the God who can become God in an even more beautiful manner tomorrow.

Energy, enthusiasm, leadership, hope: all are

the marks of a healthy personality. It is precisely this healthy personality we need to cultivate in our quest for God. And that quest, both the active searching and the receptive surrender to him who is greater than we are, is the business of religion. It is the economy of spirituality.

Repressed anger becomes apathy. Apathy murders energy and is the end of leadership and hope. And it is precisely the prayer of the inner search that leads us to see ourselves, to be in touch with that which causes apathy and blots out the attempts of God to reach us. The man suffering from the condition of repressed anger is out of touch with God because he has become a stranger unto himself.

PRAYER AND SELF-ESTEEM

The loss of self-esteem always accompanies depression. It is a most painful condition surrounded by fear; and it admits of no escape, for it dims the light of confidence from which all else flows.

As true as this is psychologically, might it also have religious or spiritual ramifications? Does the presence or lack of self-esteem have implications for prayer?

The core of faith and religion is not that we ever are or can be worthy of God's love. It is first of all that he has loved us. The main question of religion therefore is our ability to accept that love. If we are not psychologically free enough for such acceptance, then no matter how many coins the God of love showers around us our hand is closed and none may enter.

There is no greater courage than the acceptance of acceptance. This is true simply because it calls for the greatest vulnerability. Once we permit ourselves to accept that others have accepted us, then we have allowed ourselves to need them. They become part of our intimate life. It is not the same without them.

There may be relatively few people healthy enough to accept that they are loved. As old a theme as it is, the fact remains true: We are much better at giving than receiving. When we give we are in control; we are the strong one giving to the needy.

To receive is an admission that we are the needy ones. It says that we are not in control and cannot take care of this ourselves. We need others. Without them it cannot be done.

Perhaps it is a cultural matter again, but how we hate to surrender. We are no doubt more closely wed to the frontier value of rugged individualism than we know. And that becoming very much the point, how much are we in touch with it?

Why is it that so often we are willing and able to forgive others but find it extremely difficult to accept forgiveness? Long after the other ceases to flog us for our wrong (if he ever did) we continue on. Repeatedly we refuse to give the great gift of allowing ourselves to need the other.

Those small but vital signs of concern and loving respect — a card or a call, a squeeze of the hand, a small gift — we are usually willing to extend to others. But when these signs of care and love come our way, how do we react? It is no small matter to be able to admit our need of such reassurances of importance.

Often we reject those gifts given out of such love. Basically too many of us feel ourselves unworthy and will not admit that anyone else could find us worthy. We protest. We say they shouldn't have. We say they are wrong, it really isn't true. Thus we take away their right to fulfill a need and to form their own opinion of us. Who are we to say what others should think of us?

The lamentation rising all around us due to lack of love's communication is enough to deafen anyone who can hear. Actually, there are enough givers of love. The problem lies with those who are unable to accept the love given. Were we able to accept acceptance, we might be absolutely amazed at the amount of love showered around our closed-up hand all the time.

We meet frustration. We reach out, try to love, try to accept whatever comes back to us, and at times we are bitterly disappointed. We are never the same again. We have been changed. For some the experience may become a stepping stone to greater depth and wisdom; for others it may become a stumbling block to ever trusting again. One of the feelings often initially present after a destructive experience is expressed in words like these: "Who would ever love me now?"

When self-esteem receives such a blow the walls come up pretty fast and thick. They are walls we can't take down ourselves even when we get ready to do so. We cannot know we are acceptable and worthy of love unless someone loves us. And all too often we are sure that will never happen.

Meanwhile God keeps saying to us, "Abide in me." He asks us to surrender, not in fear and conquest but in love and trust. But this is precisely what we cannot do.

Surrender is not the posture of a weak person any more than listening is a sign of laziness. To surrender is to actively decide that we will allow ourselves to trust, to need, to lean and depend. This at best is half-hearted and limping if self-esteem has been injured. For how can we surrender in love if we do not believe that where we shall be led is good, that it is better than where we have been? How can we let go of the branch if we are sure that what is below is not the hand of God but the cruel rocks of impersonal fate? And how in the world can we ever accept that God's hand is loving if we don't think we are worthy of such wonderfully good news? If those experiences are not in our emotional equipment, how can they ever get projected onto God? How can they ever become God for us?

The religious implications of this process can easily be seen. Do we accept that God loves us of his own free will and choice? Can we accept that anyone would love us? Is our stance toward such relationships always that we must earn them? If so, who then is our God?

Depression always includes the loss of self-esteem. If we are not in touch with the cause of our depression, then it is inevitable that we thrust upon everyone (including God) our painful situation of not being able to accept their love and concern.

If we find that we are unable to accept, it becomes a major task of the prayer of inner search to uncover the situation, and thus at least not call it what it is not. It is not virtue to refuse to accept that God has freely loved us as we are. It is not a healthy person who refuses to accept a gift or compliment with a humble, thankful heart. It is false humility to do otherwise. We know where we are, at least at the moment, when the prayer of the inner search has allowed us to know where we are.

IMPORTANCE OF COURAGE

Over the years almost everyone has experienced the situation of needing the courage to pray. We say it in many ways. But what we are looking at here is the nature of the inner search of prayer. We will examine not so much the courage to pray as the role that courage plays in prayer.

It seems strange to me that over the years little has been said of the quality of courage needed for prayer. But maybe that is because little has been said of the distinction between the prayers of the outer embrace and the inner search. In this context courage takes on quite a different meaning.

It is one thing to have the courage to pray that God will fix what is wrong with us or the world. It is quite another to pray for the courage to see what is wrong with me, and what *I* can do to heal a bleeding planet. One approach places the responsibility on God, the other on ourselves. One is the prayer that everyone else would straighten out, would treat me better. The other humbly asks that I would straighten out and that I would have the depth to be a "healer," to treat others better so that they too might enjoy a more fear-free life.

Dr. Paul Tillich in his classic work *The Courage To Be* has said as much about courage as anyone. Passing over some fascinating history on the concept of courage, he says that courage is *the* quality of free human life. It is not a virtue among others but the foundation out of which all virtue comes.

His point is that every expression of virtue is an act of self-affirmation. Virtue is the act of embracing the beautiful, of allowing yourself to be possessed by and become, in a sense, the good that is in life. But self-affirmation is always made "in spite of." Acts of self-affirmation must be made in spite of fear, anger, or depression. If prayer is to lead us to an insight of all the "in spite ofs" in our life, then courage is an absolutely necessary condition.

Without courage there is no going on, for there is no will to go any further. When the courage of self-affirmation fails then there is nothing to stop fear and anger from dominating all. Just think of all the sterile or terribly smaller-than-necessary mind sets we are held prisoner within. There may well be no need to waste away in anger at God or anyone else if we but had the courage to see where we were coming from and deal with the situation. Are the defense mechanisms that scream out so loudly truly all that important? Could we get along without them if we could but muster the courage to affirm ourselves in some other creative way? Instead of trying to go around them, why not find a way through? But there is no going through without courage. Every act of facing, embracing and dealing with our living problems is an act of self-affirmation made in spite of all the obstacles that would impel us to evade rather than confront them. And that is courage.

Courage enables us to move on from where we are stranded. Only in courage are we ever capable of changing our basic stance toward life.

Usually a person faces life from one of two basic attitudes: trust or doubt. Of course these attitudes are learned — by repeated actions, experiences, thoughts. The quality of that life, including the concept of God, will take its form from these foundations. What is learned can be unlearned, and what has not been learned can be learned. In either case, courage will be necessary.

Some examples of the distinction between these two basic attitudes may help to clarify the issue.

There are ever so many people who could never come to admit or accept that anyone is going to offer them a loving, open hand. They just don't expect life to treat them well. Since they don't trust people to treat them well, they don't expect life to be gracious.

Have you ever known people like this? For them, gift giving and gift receiving become difficult or impossible. "Everyone has an angle. No one operates out of the goodness of his heart."

But isn't love a gift? Isn't it true that love can never be earned or owed? What have we been told all these years about faith? Faith is a free gift from a loving Father. But both of these attitudes — free and loving — are based on the premise that good not only can happen but does happen *to me*.

For those who have never learned to trust —
because life has not been kind to them — this
requires extreme courage. Nearly everyone
knows incredible stories of cruelty, misfortune,
and misery that have happened to people, even
from their earliest years. It's no wonder they can't
trust.

Recently while talking to a group of divorced
people, I mentioned how sad it is when we get
into a frame of mind that would accept peace at
any price. But usually this means no peace at all,
and the price is always too high. At times, I told
them, we might even endure physical beatings
and put up with them. We may even feel it is our
due, that we had them coming. We get told so
often we are horses that pretty soon we rush to
grab the saddle.

One young woman started to cheer. Right there
in front of all those people she was publicly pro-
claiming the absurdity of the situation. As it
turned out she knew all about hobnailed boots.

Who would blame her for not trusting? How
could she? Trusting is a skill that must be learned.
She never had a teacher. All her life the only thing
she was being taught was that she was an object to
be used.

Whenever trust seems impossible, life becomes
a fortress for concealment and defense.

It is one thing to pray to have the courage to
endure. It is quite another to pray in a way that
would illuminate the shabbiness of the situation
and have the courage to change it.

Prayer is meant to set us free, but there is no
freedom without courage. Freedom is the ability

to say yes or no, to be able to affirm self in the face of life's many situations. Freedom is the capacity to choose which way we will go, what we will do or not do. And it takes courage to affirm oneself in this way.

One wonders how many humans on the face of this earth truly believe there is anyone who wants to listen to them, who cares who they are. That others would put our growth above their own comfort should be important to us. Without acceptance of this basic attitude toward reality, life becomes hardly worth living.

There may well be more people who believe that someone else would certainly be more interested in telling them what to do than in listening to what they have to say. Perhaps far more people live without the mellowness in their lives of believing someone would want to know who they are. There are probably even more who doubt that anyone cares about them. But if this is true, then these people are grounded in doubt, not trust. And as the roots are, so is the tree.

Dialogue is a word much in vogue today, and with good reason. Dialogue is that gradual process of revealing self — a process through which trust grows and each person comes to understand the gift each is to the other. That you don't need to be afraid is its first premise. It is all right to need and to let you know that I need because I trust you will be there.

If dialogue progresses in a healthy direction, a point comes when trust so beautifies the relationship that the energies which once were predominately spent in concealment are now spent in revelation. Candor replaces secrecy. The strange thing about this is that so much of the destructive behavior manifesting itself in our society is a left-handed attempt to stave off the pains of loneliness. But loneliness is that vacuum left when intimacy is nonexistent. And it is in dialogue that intimacy grows — the kind of intimacy that slowly teaches that real trust is possible.

We want it so badly; we die without it. Yet we are so hesitant to even wet our feet in the waters of dialogue. Why is it that we are unwilling to have our loved ones die without knowing how important they are to us, but we are more than willing to let them live without that expressed knowledge?

As paradoxical as this is, the reasons for avoiding dialogue are simple enough. ''What if someone were to find out who I am behind all my masks and diversions? What if he or she truly knew how I felt and what I thought? What if he or she really knew me as I am?''

We fear rejection, so we hide. But does not all hiding show a lack of trust? And if we are not grounded in trust, then what is left but doubt?

It is hard to think of anything requiring more courage or more to the point of prayer than moving from doubt to trust. Yet if that journey is not made, what room is left for God to fill in our lives?

Have you ever doubted that someone would (or that anyone could) have patience with you? Expectation of patience is another fruit on the tree of trust. That degrading fear of being made to feel ''dumb'' is a weed that grows in the garden of doubt.

Very often in counseling sessions it surfaces

how little one person understands what the other has said or meant. This is so whether the topic is a marriage relationship, friends, or just the world in general. People seem to doubt that anyone will have the patience to explain a thought, feeling, word, or emotional reaction to them again. But doubt breeds fear; and fear erects a barrier.

For some that barrier is feigned anger at the one they don't understand and don't trust enough to say "I don't know what that means." Others put on the dunce cap and refuse to attempt to understand. But mostly fear defeats any attempt to try anything.

We are so sure in our doubt that the other(s) wouldn't have the patience to teach us how to drive, cook, play a game, or explain and discuss a book that we don't stretch our abilities. We don't try.

Like a shadow, doubt spreads. It spreads from the situation at hand to all sorts of activities we might have truly enjoyed — activities which would have profited us and others who would have learned from us. But we lacked the trust to lean on another and the courage to move from doubt to fear.

Again, it may very well be true that given persons never had anyone treat them with patience. Thus they never learned this dimension of trust. There are all too many people who have been taught by other insecure people that they are "dumb."

The need then obviously is courage — courage to deal with this situation in spite of all the fear, hesitation, and pain that may be involved. Courage to pray is one thing; prayer for courage is quite another.

History is full of those who dared go ahead. It is not so full of those who have not, for their story is too routine. Dr. Jacob Bronowski has written a history of mathematics and science called *The Ascent of Man*. Although he never mentions courage, that is what his book is about, for it outlines the "ascent" made each time people took the risk to ask questions. "Why must it be like this?" "How is this made?" "Why does this change?"

He moves from Pythagoras who discovered the relationship between mathematics and music to Priestley, Dalton, Darwin, and Albert Einstein. All of them are light throwers who stood at the edge of what was known and threw a burning light-filled question out ahead of them into possibility. That act of the willingness to ask, to seek, to embrace equals courage.

Perhaps one of the most telling points of his book concerns itself with famous Easter Island. The question he asks of this barren island with the numerous huge stone heads is not how did they get there or how were these stone monoliths carved. He doesn't even primarily ask where the original inhabitants of this island came from. Rather his question is why they never figured out how to get off the island. They remained there and became extinct.

In order to achieve navigation early man had to learn to read the stars. But one learns only through wonder, through asking questions and having the courage to go where one has not been before.

"Why does that star never seem to move?" "What part of the sky seems to remain the same?" "If I were at sea, what in the heavens could become a landmark to me? What could I sail by?"

The people of Easter Island lacked the courage to ask. They did not go beyond themselves. Because of this they did not grow. And thus they died.

But one must wonder if somewhere in that race of people some intelligent youth did not question. Perhaps the flickering of genius cast wondrous shadows on the cave of his mind and began to open a door to new knowledge. But he did not question.

He may have put words to his thoughts, but the elders laughed or told him to be silent. Maybe they even threatened that if he persisted in casting doubts on the established gods and insisted on looking wonderingly at the heavens, he would be driven from the community — to remain alone the rest of his days. What a test for his courage!

Whether on Easter Island centuries ago or on one of our continents here and now, it is by courage that we live. For only in courage do we stand before the not yet and give it life. From that "not yet" emerges either anger, fear, and depression, or hope, joy, and enthusiasm.

Prayer, that of the inner search and the courage which it demands, creates a wondrous vision — not a flight of fancy or a lazy dream but a roaring, powerful thing that sets men free. Of such things Neihardt speaks when he says man has lived to the full when he has climbed the mountain and seen the vision. It is the kind of vision seen by Dr.

King — in which men would be free and live as brothers. It is the reality of the lion who chases a terrified mouse into a corner only to find the mouse turn and attack.

True, the mouse may lose his life. But he has decided to go out raging against the night rather than whimper in a corner. Courage is the essence of the mouse attacking the lion.

We use so many props and seek so many hiding places to escape the inevitable call to courage. Desperately we search for an adequate substitute. At times we try being cute, clever, or new. But there is no substitute for courage. Until the mouse is prepared to turn and attack the lion, as improbable as that may seem, there is only slavery. For it is only in that tough, desperate decision that we learn the mouse can become the lion and the lion shrink to the proportions of the mouse. It is impossible to trick or outmaneuver the lion of depression and fear. We can rage or whimper; we can attack or withdraw. The choice is ours.

But an incredible *joy* becomes ours when we turn the lion into the mouse. There is no inner illumination greater, no matter what the price, in finding out we *can do it*. We can face that fear, say that word, say YES. That prayer can be said.

UNLISTED SAINTS

My eyes truly fill with tears thinking of the following. Across the stage of my mind plods a lady I dearly love. Her name I've forgotten or perhaps never knew. Black, she lived many years ago in St. Louis. Her weight was about 230 pounds, which made walking very difficult. My contact with her was through the housing programs. She worked so hard and walked so far to get there. For what? To fight for the few dollars remaining for the people after the thieves had stolen most of the government money coming in.

I tried one night to crawl inside her aching head, her tired feet, into her strained eyes as she looked ahead and saw miles of tortuous street stretching out before her. No fancy footwork or sly "new cure" was of any advantage. All that counted was courage — just the mental toughness to put one foot ahead of the other.

Yet she always arrived at the Community Center with a smile. There never was the thought that it was too far. Everything has its price, that's all. Either you pay it or you don't. She was willing to pay.

Her hat is what clouds my eyes. Always on her head was the same ugly, old felt hat. On anyone else it would have been a joke, but not on her. In her case it was simply all she had. On either side of the crown were two big round holes punched in the brim. At one time horse's ears stuck through those holes. And now she wore it.

We speak here of depression and prayer. Tell me of saints and "great" people and I will tell you of this magnificent woman. She is tough and without toughness nothing grows — not trust, love, freedom; not friendship, reconciliation or peace. All the eloquent sermons, pure beeswax candles, and expensive vestments are pointed in this direction. For this they exist. Yet we so often lose our way, our sense of direction. We preach finer sermons, build grander buildings, buy more expensive things and think, "We've done it. The task is completed." But, no. Is courage there? Do these things express and deepen the need for gut-level, climb-out-of-death courage? If so, fine. If not, they are nothing.

We are born so divided, so split asunder! We come into the world loving light yet clinging to darkness; we are born to give, yet we instinctively reach out to grab and possess. We arrive at a knowledge that love is all, yet must fight so desperately against selfishness. We know we come fitted for a cross, yet hate to set hand to it.

To heal the split is the goal of all living. We are born in tension with only the possibility of becoming more whole or more fragmented. But courage alone will bring jagged edge to mesh with jagged edge. Only courage allowed the tired, obese black saint to put one foot ahead of the other as the road stretched endlessly before her. That's the kind of thing it is.

Oh, but we hate to acknowledge that. "Anything — but please don't tell me I have to attack the lion. Is there any other way?"

I never knew Anita before she lost 30 pounds. Even now she is overweight. At 23, her face is exceptionally beautiful, but she won't see that. She hates herself. Her fear translates into extra weight, alcoholism, narcotic addiction, two and one-half years in a mental institution, a paranoid fear of the dark and of driving at night.

Through all of this, Anita learned to survive by running from her lion. She lied to herself so often about how she felt, why she did what she did, what she thought of herself that she lost touch with her real feelings. The mere thought of charging her lion was ample reason to eat, drink, or pop a pill.

We are born split asunder.

Something happened inside Anita. I don't know what or how, but she turned and fought. Thirty pounds came off, each one a monument to courage. She made a call, even though she was scared to death, to do something about her addiction, her expression of failure to cope with her living. Wouldn't you know the one she called was many miles away and the appointment was at night?

To run or fight, or not even try? There were many valid reasons not to show up, not to talk to a strange man about such personal problems. What if he was mean, crazy, or insensitive? What if his needs were as great as hers? Why not fix a drink instead?

But not this time. Even though it was night and the lion's eyes were burning brightly, she attacked. Anita kept that appointment and many since. That is courage. She had tried fads, escapes, theories — everything but naming and dealing with her problem.

Jesus was many things but perhaps none more than courageous. The keeping of a vision when no others understand requires toughness that must originate in a world other than this one.

So many times he spoke of what the kingdom was made. Who heard? The apostles who ran, the multitude whose blindness and lameness were healed so they could on a future day shriek, "Crucify him" — did they grasp his vision?

Perhaps not. (His mother of course understood her Son.) Yet he did not relinquish the vision. He did not abandon the giant quest or stop his ears that he would no longer hear the challenge or see the need that acted like searing fire in his Spirit.

Scripture gives but a rough sketch of the Man Jesus and his mission. Few of its thousands of words tell of the ache in Christ's eyes at the sermons that seemed ineffective or were so totally misunderstood. What did he feel when he looked out and saw starving men sleeping while he proclaimed the Bread of Life? How inexpressibly heavy was his heart when he realized that the stone walls he met could only be breached from the inside, but he was not allowed within.

Power! Everyone wanted what they thought was his power. Jesus, son of the carpenter, tell me of your utterly bitter frustration over the people's lack of grasping your offer of power. How often you must have felt like not going on. But, as with all moments when only courage counts, there was nothing to do but turn and attack the impossible odds. (So, in imitation of you, did Anita and her black sister.)

Could you have stated any more clearly the necessity of the cross for the sake of the Resurrection? There was and is no other way to freedom, growth, or holiness except through the mysterious door of the cross. Yet, then as now, the cross is avoided at any cost. And so, increased life is passed over for inconsequential reasons. "Let us first try anything, anything at all to deal with our living problems — but not the true cross."

(As one man said, if God had a forehead it

would be flat from hitting it with the heel of his hand while watching mankind and saying, "Oh, no, not again!")

On those dark, cold nights, Jesus, when you tallied up your daily efforts against results and looked forward to the next day, how often did you want to quit? How badly did you want to go home and forget this madness? As time went on you could clearly see the physical cross on the horizon, and you knew those now singing your praise would soon be pounding nails into your hands and feet. For what, Jesus, for what?

Oh, but you knew! You must have been mightily aware of your role as instrument — God's pencil writing in the sand of human time. His is the message, his the work, his the power. You knew that, didn't you? The need for and call to courage is no less, but the perspective changes. No longer are results a concern of the instrument, only that, as instrument, you do not fail.

So, the usefulness of the instrument depends entirely on the degree of death faced for the sake of life.

Steve is an instrument. He is maybe 24 and for the past year has lived at the long-term treatment center for chemically dependent persons. Steve has lived a full six months of sobriety — the first such of his adult life. He is a short man whose eyes, so newly accustomed to the living world, are as filled with excitement and enthusiasm as a child at Disneyland. He has turned and attacked with no apparent hope of victory save the satisfaction of attacking his tormentor. But in dying he has chosen life.

I was with Steve at a meeting last week. Also present was a middle-aged lady, Celeste. She too lives at long-term. It has been her home for the past eight and one-half months, although other treatment centers and institutions have been her home for over half her life. She is a beaten human being. Every inch of her torturous past is carved into her face. She has seen and felt the heel of man descend upon her.

This meeting was her first time away from the Center for all her committed months. She was terrified. Certainly everyone there knew, just *knew* how ugly and wretched she was. They surely would see her as she saw herself.

What if they were cruel or mean? What if they asked her to say something? It all would be so intolerable! Could she really — even for a few hours — leave behind the safety of the Center, where it wasn't nearly so threatening? There she was surrounded by others "just like herself" — ugly, weak losers who couldn't cope. Could she really survive that meeting where so many "decent," "good" people would be?

Celeste, weak and broken as she was, attacked. She sucked in her breath, set her face, and entered the ranks of the saints.

The meeting ended. Celeste had not spoken one word. As it happened coffee was offered at this time. Panic! "Why all this coffee?" With it would come small talk. "What if someone wanted or offered to talk to her?" Then they would know for sure. "Wasn't it enough that she died, suffered so much just to be here?"

And so there she sat, all alone, not moving, in

her threadbare coat with a child's red barrette in her hair. Her eyes, though cast down, moved swiftly back and forth, watching for someone, anyone — the Enemy — who would walk over to her and attempt to talk. Even Daniel was not so alone in his lion's den. He had confidence in God. Celeste didn't. She was sure God didn't like ugly people. And she was sure she was ugly.

If Steve had not a year ago attacked his own lion, he would not have been there. If six months ago he had not been tough enough to put away his toys in favor of life, he would not have been there. If he had not made that same gut-level, desperate decision based on nothing but blind faith and courage a thousand times since then, he would not have been there. Like the black woman, Anita, and like Jesus himself, he had many valid reasons for not going, but he had not one valid excuse. Steve was there.

Like Simon of Cyrene he bounced over to Celeste. Radiating warmth and acceptance, his attitude must have translated into safety to the terrified woman.

"Good meeting, huh?" he said. "Come on, let's get some coffee. I want to show you around this place." Though there was depth to this human encounter, she felt like Alice in Wonderland. They were two children off to see the wonders of an enchanted world. But then only those who have died know just how enchanting the world of the living can be. Arm in arm they walked. He showed her every room in the building and explained how each was used. By the time they returned she was speaking excitedly and gracing the world with her beautiful smile.

Though the work is God's, Steve is an instrument — even as Jesus was an instrument of his Father. So it will always be — those who are dead still live mightily in the currents of life they have set in motion. All are instruments in the hand of God, having to die before their life could emerge. All *had* to face the unavoidable moment when they were boxed into a corner with no way out but the way they came — even though that passage is blocked by the most fearsome beast imaginable, their own worst selves, their own darker side. Attack or die. Attack or evaporate into nothingness.

As with the rest of mankind I stand and applaud the splendid accomplishment of Celeste and Steve, of Anita and her sister. I nod my head "yes" in agreement with the theory of courage. But when it comes to my lion, to my corner, to my decision whether to attack or vanish as a person from the face of the earth the issue is clouded. Suddenly there are a great many considerations to be taken into account, making my situation just a bit different.

I want to ignore the "extenuating circumstances" surrounding Steve and Celeste. Their heroic "yes," I feel, was more clear-cut than mine. Even the temptations of Jesus himself to retreat do not compare to my reasons for backing off.

But no, we are all in the same boat. I, just as they, have the basic option of Yes or No with no compromise in between. If I would be an instrument in my circumstances, I must bear the crushing weight of God's hand as it rests on me, while leaving the consequences to him, not me. The only immediate results in which I have a real say are my own — the project of me.

I am a link in a chain, no more nor less than that. As with Steve who gave to Celeste, who will give to someone else, I am now but a point in a long series of other points. I have been given so that I may give to others, who in their turn will sing their own song. What I have to say is a river fed by countless lakes. When I open my mouth it is the black lady (and countless others like her) who speaks. People I have never met, long since dead, move in my blood and think in my mind. They live in the constant crisscrossing of electrical current in my brain. I am what I have chosen to accept. I will be what I decide to give.

Whether it is true or not that our time is more in need of prayer than any other in history could probably be argued. But to what point? The fact is we are sorely in need of prayer. Certainly we need the prayer of the outer embrace where our minds and emotions reach out to the infinite loving God with all our power. But also we sorely need the prayer of the inner search. That prayer, fortified by courage, allows us to seek out who we are so we can open the door allowing the glory of God to immerse us. From that prayer comes the fullest praying.

3.

Five Ways of Praying

Hopefully the distinction between the prayers of the outer embrace and inner search has been helpful in highlighting the relationship between prayer and depression. We are able to embrace God only with the clarity of soul and vision of heart the prayer of the inner search has allowed. There is a difference, yet the two dimensions of prayer are never far removed from one another. The line between them will fluctuate. Both are grounded in the search for God, in the loving willingness to walk with this God who has revealed himself in the whispering breeze, in the crops ripe for the harvest, and in his Son Jesus who has come to walk with us.

Here I propose to outline five "moments" of prayer. Every prayer that soars to God on eagles' wings tells us more of the eagle. Every prayer that reveals more of the eagle enables it to fly higher into the endless blue vastness who is God.

In meditating on these moments of prayer, let us not be overly concerned with whether prayer of outer embrace or prayer of inner search is involved. For even though one aspect may seem dominant in a given moment both journeys are taking place.

The five moments we will consider are:

The prayer of quiet whose main element is reflection and whose main fruit is Presence.

The prayer of listening whose main element is surrender and whose main fruit is Peace.

The prayer of others whose main element is sharing and whose main fruit is Trust.

The prayer of acceptance whose main element is seeking and whose main fruit is Serenity.

The prayer of ministry whose main element is doing and whose main fruit is Fullness of Heart.

PRAYER OF QUIET

There is a great difference between being passive and being receptive. Passivity means laying back, having zero enthusiasm. It has taken over when you are done unto and make no conscious decision about what is happening in or around you.

Receptivity is the state of being open to what is around and within. It presupposes that beautiful quality of anticipation: You are convinced that a mighty hymn is rising up out of creation and you want to be open so that you may hear.

All of us are deep, complex, hungry people searching for that which will bring fulfillment and happiness into our existence. For the demon and the angel are like the huge shapes gliding back and forth just under the surface of the ocean, as described by Herman Melville in his eerie work, *Billy Budd*. But we are that ocean. Who we are, who God is, the God above God, glides unrealized just beneath our conscious grasp. Receptivity is the openness, the willingness to allow these nebulous shapes to take concrete form that we may see and know them.

For some reason we often understand praying as talking. Many of us feel our most authentic prayer is accomplished when we are filling the mental and physical airwaves with vibrations of one kind or another. The prayer of quiet is something other than that.

In silent serenity we become receptive and thus allow the universe to reveal itself. And that revelation is the constant summoning of our deeper selves to "come in" and "be seen." The prayer of quiet allows us to embrace those shapes gliding back and forth within us.

All quiet demands reflection. The prayer of quiet is the silent openness to the messages that confront us at any given moment and the reflection upon them that we may hear their message. That revealed "word" then gently leads us both within and without.

Countless spiritual writers have encouraged their readers to look around. Jesus so often spoke of things like the birds of the air, the flowers blooming on the hillside, the fields of grain ready for harvest. All of creation was a word of God speaking to him of the Father's presence. It is not different for us.

The other night I attended a swimming party. It was held for residents of an institute for handicapped young adults. The water was blue and cool, the bodies cramped and hot, the messages to be heard in the prayer of quiet almost deafening.

For anyone who has made a habit of the prayer of quiet I suggest reflection on wheelchairs as a powerful meditation. The locker room we used was narrow; two chairs could not possibly pass at the same time. So, when one resident was changing into his bathing suit there often was nothing to do but wait for an aisle to clear so that person could proceed to the pool. It was stiflingly hot in the room. There was nothing anyone could do to improve the situation.

So much of the essence of "finding" God lies in our acknowledgment that we need him. That includes the admission of our own powerlessness. How often do we attempt to deal with our own anger, depression, violence by ourselves? If God wants to come along, fine; but the journey is not made with his power but our false pride.

A mere glance at the magnificent patience of those handicapped swimmers, their acceptance of powerlessness, spoke eloquently of our need to let go and to let God in. No one ever said that life would be easy; it wasn't even easy to simply sit there in that steaming room and wait.

The "Word" was there. Are we always receptive to what is being said?

One of the swimmers was also deaf. She was a truly lovely young woman enjoying the outing with the glee of a freed seal. To listen was to know her happiness. One of the aides of the institution was gliding her back and forth in her inner tube. Not knowing she was deaf I happened to say, "Wow, she sounds like a motorboat." His beautiful response was, "Yes, Mary is deaf. You have to look in her eyes to see what she is saying."

The prayer of quiet — its main element is reflection. If we were to quietly, receptively reflect on that young man's response, we would indeed know much of ourselves and God. "You have to look in her eyes to know what she is saying." But is that not true of us all?

One wonders at the multitude of missed communication that happens among us all — words not truly said, words deliberately misunderstood, words that fall short of the mark, words that confuse rather than clarify. Perhaps if we listened more with our eyes than with our ears, we would hear far more.

The young man's name was Frank. After he said that lovely, wise thing I watched him. He did look in Mary's eyes. He searched them with open, gentle "wanting." He truly *wanted* to "hear" what Mary had to say. He was receptive to her as a person.

Prayer and praying are not always the same. At times our prayer can be a place to hide, a way to block off all receptivity and listening. The gliding shapes remain hidden.

Reflecting back upon Frank's attitude and actions helps us to understand the kind of thing that praying should be. Are we not in the hand of God as Mary was in his? Are we any less in need of being held up, any less powerful to save ourselves than she? Do we not as desperately as Mary need and want to be heard with the same loving concern that Frank had for her?

The humbling, startling fact is that we are. Being receptive to the love and "wanting" of Frank toward Mary, it is possible to draw so much closer in the prayer of quiet to our posture with God. He is looking in our eyes. He is listening to us. He is speaking to us in all the subtle and overt ways that Frank utilized with Mary.

The prayer of quiet so often teaches that things are never what they seem. We came to help some handicapped people swim. Who would have thought we would be given a revelation of the loving God? It so happened that our main concern was not swimming but learning of God.

Debby is another aide from the institute. She is as refreshing as a summer breeze. There is a very special quality about this girl — she is a gift-giver. Her biggest gift is herself.

When dealing with the handicapped there is a tendency to first of all see *handicapped* people. This is quite different than first of all seeing *people* who are handicapped. This particular institute is for young adults. Many are young men. They are not different than any other young men. Their needs, fears, joys, and pains are the same.

In some very special way, because it is true with her, Debby is present to so many of them as a beautiful young woman who truly loves and cares about them. She is not afraid of them or of herself. Unselfishly, she gives of herself. I have seen her light very many candles in the dark night of aching loneliness.

Young people love to "horse around" at swimming parties. It was no different here. Debby was right there in the middle of it with all of them. Her actions spoke aloud: "Hey, you guys, you are just O.K. with me. We'll have a good time."

Handicapped is a strange word. For some reason we very quickly decide who is handicapped and who isn't. Perhaps the physically handicapped have an advantage over those who are not: they admit their limitations. But are we not all handicapped? Are there not multiple prisons without bars?

Reflection on the manner of Debby's presence with her guys reveals a very lovely sense of the presence of God with his people. Our own fears and lack of courage often tempt us to sculpt an image of God so far removed from the scriptural revelation that there is no resemblance. If we think that, for us, God's presence is impossible, then we will not allow that loving Father's entrance. It might be that many residents at the swimming party didn't think they deserved such attention and gift-sharing as Debby lavished on them. But how can they deny it when they see it happening right in front of their eyes? Such presence cannot be faked.

We have stated that much of depression is rooted in repressed anger. This always leads to loss of self-esteem which erases our ability to accept that God could embrace us. In our eyes we have become too "handicapped," too "crippled."

True, we are handicapped and crippled. But is there no hope? Is it true that others could not possibly embrace us if they "knew"?

That night at the swimming pool, in the prayer of quiet the lovely voice of God was saying to all who would receive it: "Do you see how this girl loves and cares and plays? Do you see how the handicapped dimension is no obstacle to loving concern? Then so shall I be with you if you but let me. If you will be touched, I will touch."

The prayer of quiet is by no means restricted to human encounters alone nor to the rather extreme situations of swimming with the handicapped. How eloquently the "scripture of nature" can speak to us of godlike living.

Perhaps there is no phrase that occurs more frequently in theology than "death to life." How often we are reminded that Jesus died that we might live, that he hung on the Cross so that he could pass through the doors of life. We are told that Baptism removes us from death to life as the ancient Hebrews passed out of slavery into the freedom of the Promised Land.

Right now the potato plants around our area are blooming. Giant water sprinklers turn the plants into deep green. It is hot this time of year and the mist blowing off these irrigation machines above the green fields makes one think of Eden as described by the sacred writers.

Within a few weeks planes will dust the crop, killing the upward growth so that the potato which is a root will grow to its largest. Then comes the harvesting.

The prayer of quiet. The prayer of reflection. How like the plants are we. Death to life. But unless death is dealt to fear, anger, unnamed hostility, and the refusal to trust another, there can be no life. Without death the crop cannot be harvested, for there is nothing to harvest.

Scores of people notice the planes dusting the crops. In fact they come from miles around to see it. No one minds. No one weeps at the death of the plants, for they know greater life is taking place beneath the ground.

We all meet trouble and tragedy in our lives. These events and situations appear with a power beyond our ability to control. Perhaps it is sickness, lack of work, trouble of one kind or another. Maybe we just call it bad luck. Perhaps it is. But, like the crop being dusted, they are the touch of death from which springs life.

A family I know sat down last night in dialogue. They were forced to since the father had recently totally lost his temper and severely damaged the house. Things around home were becoming unmanageable. The man has been out of work for many months. He is "strong," he always has "gone it alone," there never was anything he couldn't handle, he didn't need help from anyone.

But if he will not be held up by God, he will not hold up either. That in him which barred the way to surrender to God had to die. He had to be broken just as the plants had to die. Perhaps this was his time. The loss of temper with its resulting weight of shame and guilt may move him to acknowledge that this time he can't make it alone.

The fields are there. Year after year they are planted, sprayed, dusted. Dead, they then yield their harvest that others may grow strong from their journey.

All that is necessary is to look around. Look with receptivity to what is there, listen quietly to find a new dimension of the presence of God within. The sweet taste of the strawberry tells of the need to enjoy the moment; from vulnerability comes growth. There once was a Bible encased in glass near a bus stop in St. Louis. People passed it continuously. Every time I strolled past it reminded me of the loving Lord shouting out to those rushing by in such a great hurry. "Slow down, I am here, I am what you are chasing. Stop, come be refreshed."

If you were to put this book down right now and look quietly, reflectively, receptively around, what voices might you hear? The tick of a clock speaking of time, the odor of a flower speaking of graciousness, perhaps the memory of a loved one now gone reminding you of how good life can be.

It is a lovely prayer, the prayer of quiet. It is well worth the praying.

PRAYER OF LISTENING

Praying by listening presupposes someone is saying something. We can't listen to what is not said in some way. But God does speak to us. The task is to hear him.

True, God speaks to us in many ways. Certainly one of the most powerful and heart-touching is through Scripture. The prayer of quiet as I have described it entails silent reflection on the powerful messages of God all around us. What I call the prayer of listening is not only reflection but surrender to the Word of God given to us in the Bible.

Obviously, then, it is important to "read" the Bible.

There is need for clarification on this word "read." Have you ever noticed how many ways we "read" the written word? What we hear largely depends on how and why we read.

One of our teen-agers is preparing for the ordeal of testing for a driver's license. She is intently reading the driver's manual. She really doesn't care who wrote it or what the author might be saying between the lines. This isn't poetry. There will be questions demanding correct answers and that is all she cares about.

A friend of hers is very interested in motocross racing. He reads everything available concerning the building and care of racing bikes. He reads about experts in the field and is thoroughly, personally involved in all he reads. He isn't merely seeking objective answers to questions.

On the other hand, at a gift shop today I saw two lovers musing over the beautiful cards directed at depicting a moment of love. They were inspiring to watch. It was evident the cards spoke to them because he would read and show it to her; then they would nod to each other indicating, "Yes, I know what this means."

All this was far from reading for answers. Nor was it exactly like reading articles about a sport they cared for. No, this was something else. Reading words of love is not quite like anything else. There is that about it which begs to be understood, which savors of both a giving and a taking. In reading words of love the whole person is involved. Love letters don't tell you *how* to love;

they don't propagandize about how good love is. They simply state to anyone who can read what happens when you *are* in love.

Written words are translated into totally different messages depending on how they are read. A love letter can be examined by an English teacher to check for errors in spelling and punctuation. But read in this way, it is no longer a love letter. Its power to communicate is lost.

People read Scripture in many different ways. Some read it to prove someone else wrong. Others, interpreting the words to fit their own meaning, read it to justify their prejudiced hearts. It can be read as a historical document or even as a moral blueprint for correct behavior.

Let someone else argue about the rightness or wrongness of any of these readings. The point here is to see Scripture as love letters from God to man, the passionate words of a God who is perfect Love trying desperately to communicate with his contrary brood.

This is certainly not to say there is no room or need for scriptural knowledge. Obviously there is. The average person certainly needs to be more familiar with the historical context of the Bible, the forms that were employed, the symbols and myths that are in constant use throughout Scripture. Lacking this knowledge, Bible study often becomes mere talking to ourselves; all we hear are our own shadowy words.

Knowledge, however, does not replace love. To grasp Scripture it must never be removed from the context of God inviting us to a loving relationship. Knowledge is an aid not an enemy to this invitation.

And so Scripture, existing in the realm of love, always demands the surrender of the heart to the One who calls. Nearly any section of Scripture read in this light draws us closer to ourselves and God. Peace begins to pervade our existence once this surrender has begun.

Recently we buried a man who could perhaps best be described as a wonderful character. He marched to his own tune and sang his own song through life. As his daughter said, "He gave God a run for his money." But God has far more "money" than any man has "run."

The following lines from chapter six of St. John's Gospel formed the basis of the funeral homily:

All that the Father gives me shall come to me;
no one who comes will I ever reject,
because it is not to do my own will
that I have come down from heaven,
but to do the will of him who sent me.
It is the will of him who sent me
that I should lose nothing of what has been given me;
rather, that I should raise it up on the last day.

When read with eyes of love these beautiful lines call forth a willing surrender. Such a response has to be present because this verse paints such a beautiful image of God.

It seemed to the homilist that most people had a very "straight" image of God. He suggested that if God were to walk into the church at that moment, most people would expect him to look a certain way. And if he were dressed in contemporary clothes, it would be with shirt, tie, dark suit. In a word, proper.

Yet here we were burying Bill. When Bill had retired from his painting job some years earlier, they had asked him to come for a picture with the other retirees. Of course he was asked to dress "proper." That meant in suit and tie though he had almost never worn such clothes in his life. Neither had the others.

There was only one "character" who showed up in his white, paint-splattered bib overalls for the picture: Bill. That was just the song he heard and he marched to it.

". . . all the Father gives me shall come to me." Does God understand characters? Does he understand about retirement pictures and white bib overalls?

When Jesus spoke to the crowds who gathered to hear him, there must have been many characters present. Just look at his chosen apostles! And he loved them all. He did indeed understand. Jesus was so proficient with his teaching parables he must have been a wonderful storyteller as well. A great part of appreciating unique characters is seeing them in the first place. So many of the Gospel stories are filled with people who would never show up for a picture in their Sabbath best. They would come as they were and would enjoy doing so.

It seems so often Jesus worked his miracles on the Sabbath — a day that forbade even works of mercy, according to the legalists of the time. Jesus must have enjoyed that immensely. He did so not in malicious glee at another's frustration but with a twinkle that characters always seem to have sparkling in their eyes.

One day Bill was out grocery shopping with his wife. She had a cart full of groceries. Bill quietly walked up to the security guard and warned him to keep an eye on the lady with the bulging cart. "We've been keeping an eye on her," he told the young guard. "I think I might have seen her slip a jar of jelly in her purse." The guard thanked him for being the conscientious citizen he obviously was and promised to keep an eye on the lady.

Now I'm not saying Jesus would do something like that, but he did defend his apostles who were rubbing the grains of wheat between their palms to get a snack for themselves on a Sabbath day.

At any rate, reflection on Scripture with an open, honest, human mind often brings to light a face of God we never recognized before.

Death for a Christian always weds the concepts of the deceased person and "going back to God." Yet I suspect that we feel we must "dress" the person up in our minds to be proper, thus stripping him of all the character qualities that made him what he actually was in life. Why? Because of the perhaps atrocious image we have of God as being a totally "noncharacter" kind of reality who could never understand some of the zany antics that make humans lovable.

The same is true of the beautiful meditation invited by reflecting on Jesus breaking the bread of his body. If it is true that destructive behavior in its many forms is a result of a lack of genuine intimacy in one's life, then this meditation is for all of us. Again, it must be read with the eyes of love.

We all desire intimacy or closeness so very much. But what is this closeness? Of what is it made? How does it come about? What does God in Christ have to tell us or teach us about this basic element of human life?

We tend to think of closeness as a "thing," something that stands there against us, something we can see and objectify. Very possibly closeness is the name of an exchange. If the exchange is not or will not be made, then our spirits never know the freedom of trust, the security of knowing we are vulnerable and it is all right to be so.

The nature of the exchange can be seen so clearly in a summer rain. The rain falls. It doesn't safely pick its way, it doesn't check to see if all is safe or not. It falls in open vulnerability.

The grass becomes green, the fields ripen, the air is swept clean. Which part of all this is due to the rain and which to the earth? Where does one stop and the other begin? Is the freshness and greenness of the grass to be attributed to rain or soil? The truth? It is due to both. An exchange has been made. The openness of the earth receives the vitality of the rain.

And so we humans make exchanges. Gate by gate the defenses come down. Not an interchange of one sword for another, what is exchanged here is the key to the very heart of the castle of our lives. When that exchange is made closeness is born. It can be in no other way.

Fear, anger, depression, alienation — all these are opposed to closeness. All come into being by the inability to exchange trust for trust, risk for risk. Fear and frustration are the afterpain of gates remaining locked; closeness is the mellow glow when the gates were opened. The one who stood without could come as poet or pirate. That is the risk. And when this person comes as poet, there is closeness.

We all hunger for this closeness, yet many of us are locked up by the fear of risking the exchange. But only those who do dare such a risk could ever possibly know what Jesus meant when he said, "Take and eat, this is my body."

When read with the eyes of love, this whole passage becomes a most moving action, a process. It is Eucharist — as a *verb* not a *noun*. Eucharist happens.

"Take this, all of you" — you who may or may not believe, you who are locked in the dark, angry prison of depression, you who have given up hope, who have lost the decision to make options in your life. "Come to me all you who are weary." Come to me and I will give you my body and blood, and together we will find rest. I want to exchange with you. I give you my desperate love for you, I give you who I am, my presence. I am the voice speaking from the burning bush in the presence of Moses. I will be with you always. All this I give in return for your openness. As the fields open to the rain, trust me. I do not come as pirate. I am poet who comes to see and touch first of all what is good in you, that which is beautiful. Together we will then touch and heal what is broken. Trust me and I will trust you. "Come to me and I will come to you."

The apostles who heard these words certainly didn't grasp what he meant. They said yes, then went out and fell asleep. They said, "We will be with you," then all ran away. They too wept and begged for closeness but didn't understand about the exchange. And so, at the moment, they didn't make it. And they never found it — until they surrendered!

About five minutes ago a woman interrupted my typing. She stopped in to tell me of an event in her life a few days ago. She was having a serious disagreement with her husband over the behavior of a son. These two parents were split on how the situation should be handled. The friction has been going on for months.

Then last night there was a breakthrough. While in the car she reached over, took his hand, and said how much she loved him and *knew* that he loved both her and the son. The rain *fell,* the earth stood open to receive what came from heaven, the grass darkened green.

"This is my body." Verb, breakthrough, exchange. Significantly, that exchange is offered right here, right now — not to "them" at some future time but to us here and now.

A favorite meditation of mine has always been that of Jesus weeping over Jerusalem. Have you ever felt taken for granted? Have you ever experienced that unique pain of too much tenderness — of loving someone so very much and having to endure that person's deafness while he/she slides from hurt to misery to absolute heartbreak? Perhaps all of us have at some time wept on our mountain high over Jerusalem.

Every Christian knows that Jesus died on the Cross atop a hill. To be sure, we know that hill as

Calvary; but there are many hills upon which lovers die. Reading that passage I often feel that Jesus had died before he ever climbed Calvary; in a very real way he died on that hill above his beloved city.

Without too much trouble, if one will so pray, the mind of Jesus can be entered into here. Jerusalem was the Holy City — the city of endless longing for all devout Jews. How he must have loved her — her tradition, her symbolism, her people. Looking out over the city, in his mind he must have entered those streets, listened to the busy chatter in the marketplace, watched as the children played in the sunlight and neighborhood characters lived their song. He probably saw the smoke from the magnificent temple rise to heaven as the sacrifice was offered his Father. He saw, and he knew.

Yes, he did know. He knew the temple would be destroyed and with it the children in the afternoon light. The women would wail and the men would be crucified. Desperately he wanted to avoid that, wanted them to come to the fount of living water so that they need not die in the cruel desert of their own souls. He wanted them to come to him that their loneliness would be healed; for without him they would meet one another and their wounds would only become more angry.

"As a hen would gather her chicks beneath her wing would I gather you, but you would not." Who cannot relate to that? When read with the mind of love, how close we can draw to that heartbroken stranger — all prophets are strangers

— agonizing on that hill above the city that would not recognize its own time of deliverance.

The prayer of listening is the prayer of surrender. It is not a mindless giving up but a loving giving over of the powers of the soul unto a loving, beneficent God — a God who says through his Son, "Come to me, all who are weary and heavily burdened and I will give you rest."

To hear, all we need do is listen.

PRAYER OF OTHERS

There was a most strange conclusion to a homily I recently heard. The homilist was speaking of the need to say what we have to say. Why wait? How many of us have within us the stuff to make others rich, but we decline to say it. We hide it — hide it till often it is too late.

After making this point he told the congregation, "We are going to stop now for a few moments. Most of you are here with someone in your family or a friend. All of us are here as brothers and sisters in Christ. So right now I am going to give you all the time for you to say something to that person you would like to communicate with. If you have something to say, say it now."

At first it was rather quiet — almost tense. Seldom are we ever asked to do anything personal in church, anything that requires taking down the barricades, saying anything of who we are. There was no question that there was much to be said. What was at issue here was the freedom and ability to say it.

A few whispers started here and there. In a very short time the church was full of the most appropriate church music anyone ever heard: people sharing.

The looks on the faces of the crowd told their own stories. Many eyes were either full of tears of joy or the look of astonishment. So clearly they said, "No kidding! I didn't know that! I had no idea you felt that way!" It seems so often we presuppose we *know* that the other knows where we are. We are so *sure* that others must know we love them, or want things to work out better, or need them, or are sorry. But how often those presuppositions are false. They don't know. And so often we don't know.

When that sharing was finally over there was a totally different atmosphere in the community. It was more open, more real. There was a far different quality of presence because the prayer of the other had been prayed.

The simple truth is we need one another. This is such an old saying it runs the risk of becoming a cliché. It is a truism. But truisms become such because they are true — in such deep ways we forget they are true.

We began these pages talking of depression and its constant companion, anger. But if the anger is hidden under some protective cloak, how are we to find its real name? How do we get in touch with what or who we are really angry at? Prayer and praying become an essential element here, especially the prayer of the other. For it is in dialogue, in communication, in trustful sharing with one another that successive layers of blinding rock are scraped off, so giving the courage and power to see what is going on inside us.

The key word here is trusting. But how can we learn trust except by trusting another? And how can we trust others if they do not prove themselves to be trustworthy? Such a process cannot unfold without the prayer of the other.

Atmosphere is an element we are most certainly talking about here. Though a nebulous word, it's as real as a rose or a table. Upon entering a room or encountering a group of people, we sense it immediately. The very air of some gatherings breathes hostility and tension. Others carry within them the essence of trust, of safety, and gentleness. Some situations cry out, "Cover up! The demon is here and will brutalize you." Others softly coax, "Come out, unfold, all is safe here. There is room to bloom."

Healing happens not so much as the result of a technique or formula but within an atmosphere of loving communion. It is within that atmosphere we learn we are O.K. people, that we have something to say and people not only will listen but need to listen. We learn in a trusting, loving atmosphere that certainly we can do things. In fact we become positively creative. Creativity, after all, is mostly just the freedom to allow the multitude of forms, shapes, colors, and sounds that glide around inside us to emerge in some way or other. Those shapes are in us all. What is not inside us all is the freedom to let them out. We are afraid that they are not there, they are not good enough, or we fear that we will be laughed at.

But then comes someone, a Don Quixote person, who tells us over and over (as in the wonderful play *The Man of La Mancha*), I *know* what I see and you are not Aldonza the woman for hire; you are Dulcinea, you are my lady. In the play Don Quixote repeated that so often that the lady came to believe it. And when she believed it she *became* the Lady Dulcinea. The man of La Mancha created such an atmosphere of wholeness that she became whole, she became who she truly could be.

But atmosphere is like sunlight; it doesn't happen without the sun. So too, healing atmosphere doesn't happen without people. Without Don Quixote, Dulcinea was Aldonza. Without the mirror there is no reflection.

The prayer of others — which is fed by the prayer of quiet and the prayer of listening — is the process of becoming a kind of Don Quixote mirror. But no mirror can remain clear when people cast shadows upon it. It is only a matter of time till it becomes completely darkened.

There are countless indications that the prayer of others is present in our world. Its power is stupendous. In almost every parish, or within reach of every parish, one can find a prayer group, charismatic or otherwise. These groups are made up of people who strive mightily in the Lord to create an atmosphere of openness and trust. In their midst you don't have to be afraid. Theirs is not to compete, and honesty rather than deception rules their actions.

At their sessions we learn who we are and how to live. We learn to be the kind of people we are. Many voices join in this teaching process — the voices of utter failure telling of spiritless living and an increasing number of Don Quixote voices saying "bloom." Prayer groups are but one.

Recently I initiated a new youth group. This one is different in that there are no officers, no dues, no bylaws. The purpose of the group is to learn to be a family. Each week two persons volunteer to "take" the next week's meeting, which means to prepare something on a relevant topic. More than anything else it is just a jumping off point for the prayer of others.

Last night the group met. The kids started showing up around 7:30. We just sat on the grass, talking, singing songs. For everyone who arrived there was a big hello, a greeting. That in itself was significant. How many meetings had these kids previously attended where no one even said hello? They were not seen. So an atmosphere imperceptibly but surely began to form, like the glow of a warm fire.

Presently the two who had volunteered for the meeting started talking. The beginning flowed from the togetherness, naturally. No one rang a bell, called the meeting to order, or read the roll call. This was informality at its best.

The two read the *Desiderata* and spoke just a little on the need to like yourself if others are to have a chance of liking you. Then they asked a question and were themselves the first to answer. The question was: Why are you here tonight?

The two leaders set the atmosphere. It was amazingly honest, joltingly real. In the whole group of some twenty-five people there was only one who decided not to share. That decision was honored without comment. Amazingly, everyone — from a seventh grader to the mother of several of the teen-agers — answered in the same way. Basically it was the need to want to know others, to have others know who they were, to feel and be close, to learn to trust and not be afraid.

In a different terminology you could say they were there to learn the prayer of others.

Once everyone had his/her turn to share with the group, someone made a further suggestion. Many of these people had gone to church with each other for five or six years, had gone to school with one another even longer. Very probably during those years many things had been left unsaid. They had never prayed the prayer of others. They didn't know how. No one had ever taught them, the atmosphere had never presented itself. They had never met Don Quixote.

What followed was extremely touching — especially to anyone who can see beyond the now to the future and who knows the vital importance of learning the skill of praying with others. Destructive behavior, whether it manifests itself in violent divorces, alcoholism, drug addiction, apathy and depression, vandalism and pure squandered potential, does not happen when prayer of the other is present. As long as one is in the way of such prayer — and the supporting kinds of prayer that accompany it — there is always at least one leg in the life raft.

Persons moved from one to another, imparting their gift of truth. It was hard not to see them as life-giving bees moving from flower to flower, taking the sweetness from one and giving it to another. Faces glowed. Who would have guessed the wonderful gifts they were to one another? No one would have — until the prayer of the other was prayed.

From the prayer of the other we learn trust. Only in trust are we ever willing to exchange sword for key. Without trust we would be fools to do so. With no exchange each one of us must hide away within our barricaded fortress, whose atmosphere will literally kill anyone who stays there long enough.

Another incident which beautifully illustrates the power for human growth and goodness involved in this willingness to be with others happened within the realm of sports.

An avid amateur runner told me of the rather frequent races that are staged here and there for the enjoyment of such runners. He told me so many people turn out for these races, and they all know that only a few have any real chance of winning. But the whole point is they don't show up just to win, but for the sheer joy of running.

It seemed on this given day two runners who had never met each other began the race together. For a number of miles they ran stride for stride. After eight miles they were still side by side. Who would win? Which one would outdistance the other?

Most people have a fanatic drive to win. But winning has different meanings to different people. These runners, who before the race were strangers and still had not spoken a single word to each other although they had certainly been communicating, joined hands and crossed the line together. In all truth they were both winners.

Actions flow from attitudes. Attitudes are

formed in specific atmospheres. That act of coming across the line together was a clear manifestation of certain attitudes, generous, healthy, whole attitudes. They had run their race and had no need to beat down each other. Their goal was not to eliminate the other but, as they got to know and respect each other through the race, to enhance and ennoble the other. And so they came across the line together.

The prayer of the other is a prayer of sharing where trust is the atmosphere breathed. It says very clearly, "Bloom! It is safe here."

PRAYER OF ACCEPTANCE

Just as the prayer of listening presupposes a willingness to hear, so the prayer of acceptance presupposes a willingness to seek. Those who seek and know what they are looking for shall find. This prayer concerns itself with what one prayer group calls "God-touches."

God-touches are exactly what the words signify. They can and do happen at any time. What we must ask is how open we are to them and how capable we are of accepting them. Any experience of beauty is a God-touch. The greatest God-touches are those experiences of loving and being loved.

To be sure, the world is full of deceit and injury. But as the lovely poem *Desiderata* tells us, we should also be alive to the love in the world which is as perennial as the spring. The prayer of acceptance is the prayer of openness to the ever reborn song of love.

Not too long ago I had the good fortune of

seeing *Peter Pan*. Now I am not brave enough to simply go myself since it is a "child's film." Instead, what I did was finagle several companions to go with me. Gretchen with the golden hair is nine, Erin is also nine, Toddy is six, and Cara five. It was my great good luck to be seated between Toddy and Cara. Both in themselves are God-touches — the way they think, their manner of speech, their openness and incredible imagination.

At a certain point in the movie it got kind of scary. Who knew for sure if Captain Hook was going to finally get Peter as he flitted around? Right in the middle of that horrifying possibility a tiny voice to my right said, "Can I sit by you?" It was Toddy. Sit by me? He already was. How close can you get? Well, closer than he was.

Faster than Tinkerbell he was up on my lap pulling my right hand around him. Maybe if he felt safer, Peter would too.

It didn't take long before Cara had the same feeling. Being afraid for her flying hero, she felt afraid for herself. Pixie that she is, effortlessly she climbed aboard on the left side. There we sat for the rest of the movie, each one's head resting on my right and left shoulder. From that moment on I saw no more of *Peter Pan*.

Perhaps some of you have heard the haunting, moving song from Isaiah where Yahweh proclaims that he will bear us up in the palm of his hand. There we will find shelter, there we will be whole. It is one thing to know the notes and words of the song, quite another to enter into the emotional content of what the song proclaims. But somehow the absolute trust and gracefulness of the attitudes of those two God-touches in their request and willingness to draw close seemed to me what the song was about. If only in such attitudes we could draw close to the God who also would hold us close anywhere we wanted to sit — in his hand, lap, or heart. There is very little in my remembered experience as a human being that gave me such a sense of the nature of the Christian religion as that velvet soft voice saying, "Can I sit by you?" even while its owner was moving into safety — so sure was he of the answering response.

We cannot accept if we do not seek. But we cannot find if we know not what to seek or where to seek. And the God-touches are so plentiful all around us.

Moses knew a lot about God-touches. Without getting too technical it is fascinating to learn that the best scholars tell us that the "name" God gave himself through the burning bush was not a name at all. The words indicate a promise that this God in all his power had chosen his people and would be with them forever.

The name Moses brought back to the people was Yahweh. But Yahweh is not a name like John or Mary. Dr. Martin Buber, the brilliant Jewish scholar, speculates that what makes the most sense to him, having an intimate knowledge of ancient languages and also being a man of immense faith, is that what Moses heard was a primal expression of an overwhelming presence. Rather than report that God revealed himself as a person with the name of Yahweh, Moses, according to Dr. Buber, probably heard something like the utterance, "Oh He!" (Remember, Moses was overwhelmed by what was happening — a God manifesting himself through a bush that burned but was not consumed.)

"Oh He"? What in the world does that mean?

Have you ever visited a maternity ward? Have you seen the faces, heard the sounds? Primal noise. Primal communication of sound. Even before a name is given to that precious newborn another sound is heard: the "ohhhh . . ." of a father and mother as they see their child for the first time, perhaps at the moment of birth itself. About all they can say, which is everything, is "Oh, look, look, look who it is. It is he. Or it is she. The One — the One is here." (This is much like Moses is thought to have spoken.)

Some words are work words. They are used to describe or question or clarify. They indicate a certain level of existence where the object considered is under control. And that is precisely because it is an object. It is "over there," an object. We can then look at it, inspect it, touch it, analyze it. But we are doing unto it.

There are also ecstasy words. They too indicate a certain level of existence. They emerge when what is spoken of is not studied but entered into. Under control here is not the "I" but rather what is being experienced.

At such moments there are no attempts to describe, analyze, or question. All one can do is accept, surrender, and utter some such primal sound as "Oh He."

As true as these deepest of God-touches are of

birth, so are they of death. Grief and wailing are primal sounds. They name without specifying. Several times within the past few months I have heard such wailing. Twice I have heard it in wives who had suddenly and violently lost their husbands, and once in a family who lost their nine-year-old boy through drowning.

There were no real words, no names, only primal indications of immense experiences that expressed the sensation far better than any descriptive word could. These sounds were not aimed at describing the experience, they *were* the experience in the form of sound.

These people had lived with the now deceased. They had shared their lives with them, become part of them, partners. They were not object to one another, but subject. One could not be touched without the other being affected, for in all truth they were not totally separate. As one of the widows said, "Part of me died with him. It will never live again."

There are lovers who understand God-touches in such deep ways. And perhaps there is no better word to indicate the breadth of this love than "temple." For lovers, the other becomes a temple of God, a burning bush, a "place" from which the presence of God invites and gives. As with all genuine lovers there are indeed primal sounds, noises that precede the names by which we objectify our experiences. A mother holding her infant, the father at the casket of his drowned son, a man and woman who have fought their way through all the obstacles of trust and have finally arrived at the truth when they can be present to one another — these are all moments when being known is far more important than hiding. At such God-touch moments it is not so difficult to consider the meaning of Dr. Buber's supposition that what escaped the heart and lips of Moses was not a word-name but a primal sound indicating the overwhelming experience that Moses knew God was present.

There are many different degrees of God-touches, obviously. Some, such as the climbing aboard of Toddy and Cara, can teach much but do not necessarily descend to the level of primal experiences. It is not that God cannot be found there or that the prayer of acceptance cannot be prayed at that moment. But it might well not be the deepest level at which we can find God. Deeper levels can be frightening. We never want to be out of control or surrender to an experience greater than ourselves. So we shy away from them. When we can't avoid such moments we tend not to go back to them — refusing to reflect on them — and so we never learn from them. God can touch us in both joy and pain. The task is to be open to whatever way his touch comes.

If we fear being out of control or being captured by the greater than ourselves, any contact with God is just that. We cannot look upon the face of God and be in control.

PRAYER OF MINISTRY

The prayer of ministry obviously is typified by doing. Yet all doing is not ministry. The main point to be made about ministry praying is not what you give but what you receive in the giving.

It has to do with the awareness that there is most certainly more to be gained, more to be learned from active ministry to and with others than given or taught.

Have you ever looked into the face of someone who is absolutely candid? It is hard to explain this mystery exactly, but in some marvelous way those few, gift-giving individuals are transparent. It is not that you see through them, but somehow you seem to be looking into very clear, deep water. The inability to plumb the depth has not so much to do with the clarity of the water as it does with the lack of ability to see.

Conversely, what does one see when looking into the face of someone who lacks candor? What is it that is seen? What is the wall that prohibits transparency?

I hope it is not too simplistic to suggest that transparency emerges because there is nothing to hide. When there is nothing to hide, there is nothing to stop the view of another from coming in hospitality and staying as guest in that spirit. And in this there is no vulnerability. For does not vulnerability arise from the fact that what is hidden might be discovered? But again, there is nothing to hide here. The locked, hidden doors have been pried open, the haunted house de-demonized. Fear and anger that so often cause the depth to appear surprisingly near the surface of one's spirit have been faced. Thus they do not become obstacles.

So it is with those not transparent at all. What is seen when the depth rushes up to block passage is unmet, undealt with character defects. It is the fear, anger, jealousy, insecurity — all the rubbish which can so clog the spiritual ventilation of the soul — that not only prevent anyone from seeing or coming in but also (and this is proportionately true) keep us from seeing into anyone else in that area in which we are blind. We can lead no one where we ourselves have not gone.

What we are speaking of here are saints. They are the ones who most clearly exemplify that marvelous and rare condition of transparency. They are like the Master; they have perservered in their way of life long enough so that their way truly becomes their life, not a part of it. They are the ones who have made a total exchange of what needed to die in them so that what groaned to be born could emerge from the womb of life. There is no other way but the exchange; we cannot have both. The other side of the river cannot be gained without risking the swift current. We cannot have freedom from fear unless it will be faced; there can be no "purity" of communication without the risk of dialogue; those who would not continually be slave to anger in any of its manifestations from rage to depression cannot find serenity without naming their anger. And so it goes. Transparency is the lovely mellowness of having nothing to hide.

But "saint" is a confusing word. Few indeed would consider themselves saints or even aspire to be. Start talking about the saints and the click-ing sound of turnoffs becomes almost deafening. What is so sad about that is not just that all of us cannot perhaps be those kinds of "saints" but that all too often we cheat ourselves of so much of the transparency and peace that could be ours.

Saintliness is a matter of degree. A St. Joseph, St. Theresa or a Mother Theresa might have been gifted and earned transparency to an amazing degree. That does not mean the rest of us can have none of it. In fact it might well mean we can have as much of "it" as we are willing to pay for.

Pay what? What does it cost?

If it is true (and the various kinds of praying we have suggested here will allow you to listen if it is true for you or not) that this inner peace comes from the conquest of anger, fear, hostility — so that they can be exchanged for a more creative way to live — then the main road to both saint-hood and free human living is the same. Out-of-control character defects are incompatible with holiness for the same reason they are contrary to human happiness: they block out God and bottle up creative energy. Deep transparency is the mark not only of the saint but also the successful human being.

That is the price — the willingness to put away games and destructive living for the sake of trans-parency.

Perhaps some concrete examples will both clarify the point and indicate the necessity of the prayer of ministry.

As strange as it may sound to those whose ears are not used to hearing it, peace, transparency, successful living require that we recognize the gift that we are in others' lives. We must accept the truth that others need us, and also of course that we need them.

But how are we ever to learn this in such a way

that it becomes integrated into our lives if we are not involved in giving to others that we might receive? We cannot have if we do not give.

Reconsider, for a moment, the swim for the handicapped that was mentioned earlier. Frequently those who volunteer for such a project not only feel they have little or nothing to give but also think that no one would want to bother with them anyway. They, as most of us, take so for granted the obvious gift that they can walk, talk, move about. They could and can get in and out of a pool anytime they want. Before they even move a finger they are tremendously gifted simply because they can.

A marvelous revelation begins to pervade the face and presence of these volunteers as they begin to *see*, perhaps for the first time, just how much others do need them and how much they do have to give.

This is true especially if the experience deepens past the mere physical expression. Usually it does. For what the volunteers discover is not that they are helping crippled people but also friends. They come to believe that it is not just their healthy arms and legs that are appreciated but *they themselves*. For once you begin to love, just anyone won't do. It is the special "you" that you are which makes the difference.

Carrie is a beautiful young blond volunteer who helps the swimmers. Ken is a fine, handsome resident of the institute. They are approximately the same age. Ken has been in a wheelchair all his life. His speech is limited to a few words although his spirit and intelligence are limitless. He is as normal as any young man in his early twenties can be. And he has come to love Carrie very much.

The night I was there Ken looks around immediately and begins shouting, "Where is Carrie?" Anyone won't do. He isn't just looking for help, he is looking for Carrie. If there were some instrument that could measure joy from one to ten, Ken would register eleven when he sees her. She is always there.

I'm not sure how much Carrie knew or knows what a gift she is. But she would have to be as deaf as the Rockies not to know what she means to Ken. There is no way she could come away from that ministry not knowing she is special. If some such negative thoughts about what she has to give others have been an obstacle to her transparency, she has a powerful force in Ken to help her over it.

But how would she ever know Ken or the gift that *he* is to *her* if she did not extend herself?

Examples of this nature abound. We all know of them. Nearly every one of us could cite how glad we are Mr. or Mrs. So-and-So got involved with this or that activity which helped us so much. We always knew they had so much to give.

We are all very sure about what others have to give. We are not always so sure about the gift that we are to others. And there is no better way of finding that out than by giving the gift of ourselves to others.

Anger and lack of transparency often are the reasons why some people become loners. They claim they need no one. Strength means to go it alone; and *they are strong.* They say it's acceptable for them to give but not to receive.

Where do we ever learn gracefully to receive?

Again let us return to the swim for the handicapped. Those who gift us are the ones who show by their brokenness what it means to pass from death to life. They are the ones who heal us, and the ones we help heal are those we allow to see our need.

The residents of the institute cannot change into or out of their suits; they cannot move to the pool's edge themselves, nor can they get into or out of the water alone. In fact, very few could be in the water alone without immediately drowning. With them there is no such thing as a loner. That is a game they just don't have the luxury of playing.

Yet with all of them there is an immense graciousness in accepting the help we have to offer. They are consummate teachers in the rare art of joyfully receiving. They show neither hostility at their need to receive nor do they show some kind of pseudoworship for those who help them. There simply is a reality that must be dealt with here. It states, "Look, I want to swim. I can't do it alone, so I will allow you to help me and we'll both have a lot of fun." Simple — in the way that transparency is simple, in the way that God is simple.

How easily and pervasively the loner syndrome seeps into our lives. When we are hurt, in need, angry — or even joyful — it is indeed a temptation to hide it. "Go it alone," we say. "We'll weather the storm by ourselves." When it has passed, *then* we can tell another, "Hey, know where I was? . . ." But then it is too late to share it. It is past. So often we say we want someone to be "there" with us. Yet frequently we never tell anyone where we are so they can be there with us! Rather than be "with" someone we play the loner.

There is no thought here that this is easy. It hurts to have to work at the living problem of feeling we are not worth anything or to give up the loner attitude for a cozier life "with" someone. But that is not to say the other way is free.

As hard as it is to creep from behind some protective wall, it is even harder to stay behind it. The alternative to coming out from behind the wall is to admit to and live with the feeling of worthlessness. The option of allowing someone into our life is to forever ride the range of life alone and desperate. There is no free way. Both ways hurt.

This is not to say it happens all at once. The most important thing in going a thousand miles is taking the first step. It's a matter of creeping. Seldom are we set free of some slavery all of a sudden. What sometimes looks like a sudden change is the result of tiny decisions made slowly one after the other until it becomes possible to "all of a sudden" step forth.

Beginning is what counts. Taking that first tiny step that will lead to another, and then another until freedom is found in transparency is all-important.

The inability to accept limitations or live up to potential are two main reasons for a lack of transparency. There is no one who lives without limitations and few who live up to their realistic potential. Our task is to find and accept both.

There are the obvious (but not necessarily accepted) limitations that arise from making our primary decisions of life. Certain disaster is begun when these decisions are neglected.

An undertaker who begins to resent the dead had better either change his decision or accept the reality of his profession. The same is true of a priest who starts to resent people who come for help, or married people who rebel at the limitations involved in that way of life.

Limitations are present in every situation of life. We see them, for example, in our love for others, the people with whom we live. If our limitations can be changed, we should change them. If not, there is nothing to do but accept them. And the more they can be accepted with a loving surrender, the more serenity emerges.

There are other limitations that exist even on a deeper level — those that simply have to do with being a human being. The great limitation to life is death. Yet there are many who do not accept even this.

There is a limit woven into the very fabric of loving. The deeper the love, the greater the desire for union. But also the deeper the love, the more awareness that the closeness can never be close enough. That too must be accepted.

To embark upon the path of prayer and praying that would illuminate the inner temple of our spirits so that transparency might grow also ushers in a very real limitation. Growth is a hunger. To know growth or freedom is to know there can never be enough. There is a limit to where we can be or go tomorrow. There is a limit to the speed with which depression can be left behind.

But to grow in the dimension of accepting limitations is to come to the acceptance of journey or process. Time doesn't matter all that much. What counts is the direction we are going, the path we have chosen. If the direction is true, then that's all that matters; for there is no end to where we can go. And that will come in its own time.

Consider again our swimming party. To see the joy radiate from those faces is to seriously question who is handicapped and who is not. If limitations are an obstacle to joyful transparency, then why are the handicapped not the most unhappy people on earth? And this most certainly is not the situation.

Here, in the prayer of ministry, one learns to accept those limitations which cannot be changed. That is the source of joy. Once that acceptance takes place, then that person can get busy about actualizing what he does have instead of moaning about what he doesn't. It is then that persons discover, no matter how limited, just how rich they truly are.

It is correct that Mary can neither walk, speak, hold a comb, nor brush her teeth, and she is also deaf. But it is also correct that she can enjoy the water, feel its coolness, laugh at all the fun around her, and know the love of Frank who says, "Look into her eyes to see what she is saying."

But who would know that, and who would learn the marvelous lesson of Mary without being there to witness it? Such is the gift of those who are gifted when engaging in the prayer of ministry.

Better than anything I know, this parable about the two bodies of water familiar to Jesus states the case of the prayer of ministry:

"One is fresh, and fish are in it. Splashes of green adorn its banks. Trees spread their branches over it, and stretch out thirsty roots to sip of its healing waters. Along its shores the children play, as children played when Jesus was there. He loved it. He could look across its silver surface when he spoke his parables.

"The river Jordan is fed with sparkling water from the hills. Men build their houses near to it, and birds their nests; and every kind of life is happier because it is there.

"The river Jordan flows on south into another sea. Here is no splash of fish, no fluttering leaf, no song of birds, no children's laughter. Travelers choose another route unless on urgent business. The air hangs heavy above its water, and neither man nor beast nor fowl will drink.

"What makes this mighty difference in these neighbor seas? Not the river Jordan. It empties the same good water into both. Not the soil in which they lie, not the country round about. The difference is this. The Sea of Galilee receives but does not keep the Jordan. For every drop that flows into it another drop flows out. The other sea is shrewder, hoarding its income jealously. Every drop it gets it keeps. The Sea of Galilee gives and lives. This other sea gives nothing. It is named the Dead Sea."

LORD, HELP ME TO STRIVE DAILY TO BE A MORE LOVING, CONCERNED, AND SHARING PERSON. IT IS IN GIVING THAT I, TOO, WILL

RECEIVE.

By enriching the lives of others I find my own greatest fulfillment. If I am willing to surrender the false ego — the little self — and lose myself in a dream, a goal, an ambition, in love and service to others, then, and only then, will I experience a foretaste of heaven.

Conclusion

And so we come to the end of these pages. Were these simply thoughts on the psychology of depression or theological speculation on the relationship between depression and prayer, it wouldn't be so difficult to conclude. Then we could comfortably close with some equally speculative wishes of good luck.

Such is not the case. This book has been about people and their pain. One doesn't quite so glibly say good luck in the face of an agonizing situation: for example, the reality of the two little boys who desperately needed to know "the neighborhood," and the equally great need for "the neighborhood" (the lady concerned) to know someone is there for her; or the anger of the alienated young man at the party and the slow, seething rage of the woman daily driving past the wet T-shirt sign. Anger, depression, the desperate seeking of freedom from depression's grip is not speculation but a flesh and blood fact.

In the face of such painful facts such people are asking, "Which way should we go?" "Where do we turn?" "What do we do now?" That is why it is not so easy to know how to conclude.

Certainly there are recommendations that can be made — concrete, practical, physical things to be done. Get a part-time job or go back to school if depression seems a constant visitor and you feel crushingly cooped up in your house. Perhaps there you'll find you have much to give and much you can do.

If you are faced with a difficult decision that seems to recur often and weigh you down, perhaps what you should do is practice Yoga. Get away from the impacted mind. Clear your thoughts, relax. Maybe what you are looking at in this situation is the need for prayer, whatever kind of praying is most suitable to you at the time.

What to do might be as easy as singing a song. So it was the other night. A whole gang of youth showed up for our weekly meeting. One of the girls, Wendy, was in a depressed mood. Her day had been bad. What she needed was to join in the singing, to hold a hand, to talk to one of her caring friends. And this she did.

Concrete, practical suggestions abound. There is successful therapy for some in writing out their feelings, or writing poems about the events that come and go in their lives. For others, dialogue with someone they trust and love is always helpful. They should join a group that has a high trust level.

For some the practical thing that needs to be done is see a doctor. Medical care or at least advice may be just the ticket.

But there is another issue at work under all these suggestions. And that issue is a "change of focus" or attitude.

Attitudes are what makes our lives to be what they are. Attitudes are the eyes by which we view the world. Outer reality doesn't change much but our perspective of it certainly does. The difference between a positive mental attitude and a negative one is not in what happens but in how we interpret what happens.

Who we are and how we handle our lives can be equated with our "focus," the way we see things. Perhaps all learning or growth is basically that — a change of focus. And that change usually happens due to a good knock on the head. We get jolted. Then we shake our heads and look again. What we find when we look a second time is not quite what we saw before the head knocking. The focus has changed a bit. We see differently. The world then *is* a little different. And because it is different we adjust and respond to it differently. It's a matter of attitude.

A lovely young woman who is walking around with much sickness in her body told me what happened at a recent meeting. While she was talking about her difficulty in accepting her illness a note was passed to her. Everyone at the meeting loved her and gave her the tenderest care and support. The lady who passed her the note had herself been laid low with a heart attack the previous year. What stood out in the note was the phrase, ". . . God is healing you *now*."

What is important is not what has happened or what will happen, but what *is* happening. God is the God of now. He is acting now. He is present now. In his love for this woman he is healing her now.

The insight she gained was touching her at *that* moment. And of course what that led to was a change of attitude.

Her body remained the same — the outer reality did not change. But she changed. She changed because her perspective of the situation had altered. There was more "space" in her understanding for other views of what was going on — not only within her but in her relationships as well.

Certainly the concrete, practical, physical things are most important. Wendy needed to sing her songs the other night. But somehow they are like the flowers that appear above ground; they depend on the roots. The loveliness of the flower does indeed motivate us to take better care of the roots so the plant will prosper. It might even encourage us to plant new flowers. But the flower appears because the roots are deep and solid. The roots of our lives are the attitudes.

To find transparency or a release from the anger-depression syndrome is to find the door to God. It is to find the very breath of God in our lives. But is that not also to say it is to operate on the attitude that *"No,* I not only don't have to be but *will not be* a doormat to be walked on"? It is to adopt the attitude that I am a gift and do have a gift that is important to pass on to others. It means accepting a life style that maintains it is not only *right* but necessary to admit when I am angry — and this to avoid an out-of-control rage which can only lead to destruction.

A deep relationship with God or personal freedom can be found only through a growth in sound attitudes.

But there is a problem here. Although attitudes are the strongest realities in our life, they are also the most subtle. Very concrete suggestions on changing attitudes can be made, but the attitude itself is of the spirit — nebulous. Incredibly sophisticated techniques (costing millions of dollars to research and formulate) are being used in an attempt to reconcile a broken marriage or family relationship. But that essential movement of the spirit which alone brings about the experience of reconciliation or freedom rises above technique like the morning sun above the earth. Technique is but the servant. It is important, but it is not the central issue.

So, on the one hand it would be easy to end these pages with a "good luck" and some practical suggestions. But this would say nothing about the attitudes that are the main concern of the suggestions.

On the other hand this book could conclude with some thoughts on attitudes without giving practical suggestions on how anger, fear, and loss of self-esteem might be displaced by better attitudes. These would make wonderful reading, but they would be of no practical use to the depressed.

Therefore let these pages end with a wedding of the two. And let that wedding be summarized in the phrase: **EASY DOES IT.**

"Easy does it" reminds us that things don't happen all of a sudden. We do not have total control over where we will be tomorrow or even an hour from now. Within all of us are powerful forces at work that tend to lead us to creative insights and freedom or that barricade the door making us slaves of a lightless house.

These forces are a mixture of our personal attitudes and the positive, concrete actions we take to improve them. Or they may be wrong attitudes and repeated actions that lead us astray. Attitudes feed on actions. They build on each other. Attitudes, like relationships, do not live in vacuums. Reversing an attitude requires positive, concrete actions that then become material for creative insights. Trust is an attitude. But we don't learn to distrust all at once any more than we learn to trust immediately after being burned. And this subtle, powerful movement back and forth within us is a constant process. We must learn to be gentle with ourselves — gentle without giving in to the cruelty of accepting destructive attitudes for ourselves. At times we will admit that this is the way it is (like being a doormat) and there is nothing that can be done about it at the moment. There *is* something that can be done about it. But that wedding of concrete and attitudinal change that brings about the liberating freedom happens in its own time. It comes slowly. "Easy does it."

What we are talking of here is the difference between passivity and receptivity, as noted previously. Passivity is retirement into self; receptivity is openness to God and our own best selves.

Passivity is the stance of one who has given up. There is no effort to deal with one's own reality. The "broken will," as we mentioned before, is the root of passivity. It says, "I am what I am, the world is what it is, and nothing can be done about it. Let happen what will happen."

Passivity marks a retreat from the tides within us — the very tides that form the attitudes with which we view and understand the world. When passivity is in control there is no attempt to understand ourselves or the mighty ways that God is calling us to a fuller life.

Depression and passivity are twins. Neither fight nor flight is thought of when they are present. Their creed is to sit down and be eaten by the dogs of war.

The difference between passivity and receptivity lies in the destination of each. Passive people are totally out of touch with their own identities. Passivity leads to nothingness.

Receptivity is passionately in touch with the deeper levels of self. It is much like the attitude of one sitting by his front door on a dark night. He knows that just beyond the door is a whole world alive with moving things. And that world is the person himself.

The door is open — an invitation to see and know and touch what is. There is no attempt to lock the door of consciousness. Such an attitude of openness can grow slowly and admit of many degrees; but as far as what we want and are trying to accomplish, the door is open.

All creativity is a matter of receptivity. Insights, deeper knowledge, transparency, freedom — all are children of receptivity. Which angels or demons will come into the light of our cabin from our own unknown darkness depends on whether we allow them entrance or not.

To ask, "What should I do?" "Where should I turn?" are questions about being led. "What road am I being led down? Where am I going? Where will it end? Where will all this lead me?"

But who knows? The journey is into the unknown. But of this we can be sure: if we try to remain receptive to that area of the deep that calls out to us from within, when it is our time, we will know. Each step will reveal another step to be taken.

Was it Yahweh who spoke to Moses from the burning bush or just the wind? Was it the God of his fathers or the god of the mountain worshiped by pagan tribes that called out? What should he do? Regardless of the voice's origin, would he possibly know how to do what was asked? "Go down into Egypt and lead the people out." Surely that was a joke. It couldn't be done!

Are we so different from Moses? Do all of us not have our own burning bush calling out to us from some incredibly deep level of our being — begging us to set ourselves free, to do what we must to throw off the chains of Egypt?

Are we not like Moses in that we don't know how to get the job done, and what practical steps must be taken? Don't we wonder, after the first step, whether the attitudinal change that both supports and enables other concrete steps will bear us up?

But just as with Moses, if we continue to remain

receptive, the signs will be there. Like deep calling unto deep, every step we take changes us. It allows the light to be cast out a bit further in our attempts to see, permitting the unseen but powerfully felt world lying just beyond our door to come into view.

In our efforts should we bear down harder or ease off? Should we surrender by accepting what can't be changed or surrender by changing what we feel can be changed? "Should I leave or stay?" "Should I speak or not speak?" "And if speak, what words should I use?"

These are difficult questions. No one else can answer for you. You will only know your answer by allowing yourself to be led, to be receptive to the authentic voices speaking to you from your own depth.

At times in our efforts to gain greater holiness we are like a worker attempting to force a drill through solid rock. How the worker sweats and the drill smokes! The harder he bears down the more the smoke. The drill turns first red, then white hot. Rock chips seem to be flying everywhere. The attitude of the situation is one of desperation and violence. It would almost seem that some kind of time limit has been set: that this sheer rock wall *must* be drilled through within the hour or . . . or what? (But what is the time schedule and who holds the clock?) "Easy does it." It the worker burns out the drill what will he work with then?

Dr. May in his book on creativity makes the point that creative insights always seem to emerge in the passing back and forth of concentration and relaxing. It isn't just a matter of bearing down on the drill and making the smoke and chips fly. That is only part of it. To coax a stranger out of our inner darkness we must leave the door open and extend an invitation. It is not a matter of outfitting a hunting party and going out to catch anything. More is caught by invitation than all the nets ever made.

Once we give ourselves permission to ease off periodically there is more room — room in the sense that there is "space" to see more of the rock wall. And, in looking, we often find it isn't solid rock at all. In fact, the wall may contain many doors — even open doors — inviting us to find a much easier way through. These are the openings that can't be seen and recognized by the worker violently blasting away with his drill.

The point is that in a way it isn't the active, conscious part of us that leads us through the Red Sea anyway. It's not so much that we forge for ourselves some grand vision that we then put into operation. What is far more true is that the grand vision, when invited and coaxed by an "easy does it" attitude, comes and possesses us. We become the instrument, the artist's brush, used by the vision to express itself. It holds us; we do not surround it. Instead of trying to diminish the vision to our size, we become part of something larger than ourselves.

"Easy does it." One step leads to another. We must allow ourselves to be gently led through the violent waters of depression or whatever. And we can be led if we allow it. From out of the deep will come a saving Word that illuminates the next step, and a vision will begin to dawn around us. We will hear, and what we hear coming from the deep, dark desert within might well sound very much like words we have never fully understood before, ''Come to me all you who are weary and heavily burdened and you will find rest.''